For Rich and Bodhi, kindred souls

ANNIE RIDOUT is the author of *The Freelance Mum* and *Shy*, founder of The Robora (online courses for women in business) and works as a freelance journalist for national news and women's magazines including the *Guardian*, *Grazia*, *Red Magazine*, *Stylist* and *Forbes*. She lives with her husband and their three children in London.

'In a noisy, opinionated world where putting yourself out there is seemingly the only way to succeed, Annie offers a reassuring celebration of shyness and the benefits it can bring us, alongside a practical guide to how to overcome the ways in which it can hold us back'

Laura Whateley, bestselling author of
Money: A User's Guide

'Not only is *Shy* a reassuringly relatable read for any of us who have ever felt lacking in confidence, it's also a practical and galvanising guide to helping you harness the power of shyness, particularly in an increasingly digital world'

Rosamund Dean, deputy editor of *Grazia*

'Mixing personal experience with expertise from clinical psychologists, Annie Ridout looks at how shyness can be, rather than a character flaw as we have been taught, a gift; one we should embrace rather than try to fix'

Irish Independent

'Full of empathy and wisdom: *Shy* is a book for anyone who has stood in the doorway of a party fighting the urge to run away. A handbook for understanding and working with shyness; perfectly timed to soothe our post-pandemic social nerves' **Rebecca Schiller, author of *Earthed***

'Finally, a book for those of us who live at the (faintly guilty) intersection between wanting to be the life and soul of the party, and not wanting to go to the party. Whether you're "truly" shy, socially anxious or introverted (or, like me, any one depending on the time of day), Annie Ridout takes several deep dives and, as is her wont, comes up with enlightening and practical truths about our too-uncelebrated people'
Robyn Wilder, columnist, journalist and author

Also by the author

The Freelance Mum:
A flexible guide for better work-life balance

shy

How Being Quiet Can Lead to Success

Annie Ridout

4th ESTATE • London

4th Estate
An imprint of HarperCollins*Publishers*
1 London Bridge Street
London SE1 9GF

www.4thEstate.co.uk

HarperCollins*Publishers*
1st Floor, Watermarque Building, Ringsend Road
Dublin 4, Ireland

First published in Great Britain in 2021 by 4th Estate
This 4th Estate paperback edition published in 2022

1

Printed and bound in the UK
using 100% renewable electricity at CPI Group (UK) Ltd

MIX
Paper from
responsible sources
FSC™ C007454

This book is produced from independently certified FSC paper
to ensure responsible forest management

Find out more about HarperCollins and the environment at
www.harpercollins.co.uk/green

Contents

Introduction

Most of us have some understanding of shyness. Perhaps as a child, we felt awkward about going to kids' parties if we didn't know anyone there. Or as adults, dread the idea of the office Christmas party and having to socialise with colleagues in a different context. It might be an invite to an old friend's wedding when we're no longer in the same social circle that sparks panic, or having to present to a room of people. Shyness may be ever-present; it may come and go. It can manifest as blushing, or make us feel unable to leave the house.

For those who feel affected by shyness, or believe someone close to them is – a partner, child, friend or sibling – it might be reassuring to hear that 57 per cent of UK adults feel shy, and that a recent UK-based study of over 550,000 people found that shyness isn't a fixed trait; it's something that varies over time based on a person's social roles. Our levels of shyness are affected by our jobs, income and family relationships – all external factors that can potentially be tweaked and adjusted.

What I find particularly interesting about shyness is that this personality trait – partly genetic; partly environmental – is largely viewed as a 'fault' and something that needs to be fixed. In fact, a quick google of 'shyness' will lead you to masses of articles on social anxiety – including a BBC article asking whether shyness is a mental health problem. Firstly, it should be made clear that shyness and social anxiety are different things. And secondly, why aren't we talking about the *benefits* of shyness?

As a formerly very shy, now just-a-little-bit shy person, I'm in a position to reflect on what I've gained from being shy – and how this in many ways led to success both in terms of my career and my home life. Being shy forced me to listen, observe, empathise, examine. Favouring quiet time meant I read a lot, I learned to write. I wonder if I would have ended up writing articles and books if I'd been outgoing as a child, and feel that I probably wouldn't.

But it did create barriers, too. For instance, I was petri-fied by the idea of public speaking and pitching for work. Perhaps I'm more sensitive to rejection. So I've had to find ways to overcome these hurdles. And I have. I'm now a published journalist – I write for national print and online press – author of *The Freelance Mum* and I speak regularly on BBC radio, TV and live on panels. I love being interviewed, and get a thrill from speaking in front of a big audience.

I'd like to show other shy people that they too can not just survive, but thrive. Being naturally quiet doesn't need to hold you back. Quite the opposite, in fact; it may just be the making of you. Being born with a propensity towards shyness can feel inhibiting but, like with all of life's challenges, it means you are forced to find ways to compensate. Perhaps that's what spurred on Beyoncé, Nicole Kidman, Rosa Parks, Greta Thunberg, Elton John, Richard Branson – all of whom are known to have been shy and yet wound up as some of the world's most impressive performers and public figures.

In this book, with the help of clinical psychologists and psychotherapists, I explore what shyness really is, and why some are more affected than others. I delve deep into my own experience of being a shy child – and how I learned to overcome the social aspects of shyness that I felt were holding me back. I speak to comedians, artists, writers, actors, celebrities and celebrity interviewers to show you that shyness can lurk in the most unlikely places. It doesn't have to be seen as a negative but, for those who feel held back by their own shyness, I've included tools for building your confidence and combating certain elements of it. It's structured as ten lessons I've learned from being shy. Here they are . . .

1

Shyness isn't a fixed trait

Shyness is when you turn your head
away from something you want

Jonathan Safran Foer

As a young child, I was shy. I'd hide in the folds of my mum's flowing skirts rather than join in with the party games. When well-meaning adults leant down to talk to me, I recoiled. I wanted to be left in a safe, quiet space and to emerge when I felt ready. Somehow, I managed to make friends, but at the centre of my social circle there was always a 'best friend' – one girl I was closest to and on whom I was somewhat reliant. She was always more confident than me. This was how I protected myself in the school playground, at parties and in other social situations: by positioning myself as her shadow. She did the speaking and then decided how the play would unravel; I followed suit. I wonder now if these best friends were mother replacements: if I couldn't hide in my mum's skirt, I'd attach myself to a peer.

Outside of that close friendship, I'd have other girls and boys I played with. I wasn't too shy to integrate, I just needed to adjust to each new environment and mingle in my own time, on my own terms. And it's this very fact that distinguishes shyness from both introversion and social anxiety. Because a shy child may desperately *want* to be part of a wide friendship group and even to be centre stage at points – I certainly did; I loved both performing onstage and in front of my friends – but they are held back by shyness.

Clinical psychologist Dr Emma Svanberg explains the difference between introversion and shyness as follows: 'Often introverts are happy in their own company,' she says, 'whereas shy people would like to be able to connect more but don't always feel able to. It's also not to be con-fused with social anxiety, which is based on a fear response rather than a personality trait.'

Svanberg's note sums up my childhood shyness. I felt like there was this confidence somewhere inside me but I just didn't know how to access that part of myself. And because I was shy, I wasn't able to express how held back I some-times felt. Shyness can make you feel quite trapped – a bit like sleep paralysis, when your mind wakes up before your body and so you feel physically frozen though your mind is acutely active. Thankfully, though, while shyness is some-thing that will always lurk within me and in some ways impact my decision-making, I'm no longer paralysed by it.

And this makes sense, as studies have proven that unlike introversion, shyness isn't a fixed personality trait.

If you're not sure whether you're shy, introverted, or socially anxious, this description from Dr Svanberg might help:

> Shyness is more like: 'I prefer to stand back and observe before getting involved' whereas social anxiety is: 'people are frightening and a threat to me/my self-esteem'. Introversion is: 'I find energy from spending time alone or in small groups', versus extroversion: 'I find energy from being with others'. Introverts enjoy being solitary and are generally more reserved. It's a different personality trait (shyness is more related to openness vs cautiousness).

According to a 2017 Shyness study: 'Shyness involves discomfort and inhibition in social situations, specifically in novel social contexts.'[1] It makes sense then, that it was at parties that I would find myself wanting to creep back out the front door, or hide with one of my parents. But an earlier study, from 2011, found that our personalities are in fact informed by experienced events and social roles, as well as self-perceptions and others' responses to our behaviour.[2] This leaves parents with two options: hold close the kid who so desperately fears new and unknown social situations, or push them a little, as this may help to lift the lid on that shyness and encourage them to adapt.

Clinical neuropsychologist Dr Ruth Erskine specialises in child psychology and says that in terms of whether shyness is genetic or learned, it's complex. After all, she says, 'You can't really separate genes from environment because genes only become active in an environment.' Some things are hardwired, though, while some things are more experience dependent. So a child might have a base level temperament and this will affect whether they are more or less sociable. 'Children have different ways of engaging with the world,' she says. 'Some want to engage, some observe, some are watchful.' She believes that while we may have inherent characteristics, they develop through interaction with other people. A basic tendency will or will not develop depending on experience.

This theory is corroborated in an episode of the BBC's *CrowdScience*, called 'Why am I shy?'[3], when Thalia Eley, professor of developmental behavioural genetics at King's College London, explains that only around 30 per cent of shyness as a personality trait is down to genetics and that the rest is a response to our environment. 'We think of shyness as a temperamental trait and temperament is like a precursor to personality,' she says. 'When very young children are starting to engage with other people you see variations in how comfortable [they] are in speaking to an adult that they don't know.'

Dr Erskine also notes the potential correlation between our position in the family and our shyness levels. For instance, might the secondborn child, who less often has the full attention of her parents, sit back and observe, while the firstborn, who is used to being at the centre of her parents' world, continues to confidently perform? This interests me, as the secondborn child – I'm the middle sibling, I have an older sister and a younger brother – as I certainly lived in my big sister's shadow; following her around, allowing her to speak for me. So the idea that this might have been a factor in my withdrawing a little, while my sister continued to be more outgoing, feels plausible. But it's anecdotal, and I have found examples of both sets of siblings where the middle child of three is more shy and where she is more dominant or confident. The root of shyness is made more complicated by the various potential causes. And most likely, it's a combination of a base level wariness, and then a particular combination of life experiences.

My parents were accepting of my shyness and managed to strike a good balance, as far as I can remember: continually offering me opportunities to integrate and try out new social activities, but never making me feel ashamed if I didn't feel comfortable doing it. But as I moved into my teens and 20s, and became independent, it was now up to me to challenge myself in terms of entering social and educational situations that filled me with dread. What I found is that while my childhood shyness was there for all to see, as I wasn't yet emotionally mature enough to mask it, I was able to do a good job of hiding it as I grew older. This meant most people had no idea that I was shy. They might have mistaken my quietness for rudeness or even arrogance. This is a common error, and worth bearing in mind the next time you perceive someone as rude: are they actually just shy? What would happen if you gave them some extra time, and cracked through that shy shell? As the author Maya Angelou wrote in *A Letter to My Daughter*: 'I am convinced that most people do not grow up . . . our real selves, the children inside, are still innocent and shy as magnolias.' And yet as we mature, it can be harder to identify shyness; maybe that's because we expect people to 'grow out of it'. But instead, it becomes buried inside and can feel like a source of shame.

Sometimes, though, the 'fake it till you make it' approach can be rather useful, because while I would spend days panicking about having to perform in front of my drama A level class or, later, present a project to my fellow students during my English BA degree, no one really knew that I was shy. Because they didn't know, they treated me like a confident person; not someone who needed extra nurturing, and this meant that in time, and with the right tools, I came to adapt to the person they thought I was, rather than the person I felt like inside. And this mask soon morphed into the real me, as I entered my 30s and realised that my shyness had truly begun to disappear. I felt confident and bold.

It's important to note, though, that there are different levels of shyness. Psychologists Ray Crozier and Lynn Alden explain in their book *Coping with Shyness and Social Phobia* that most of us are shy at least some of the time but can deal with it.[4] For others, shyness is something they would change if they could. And then, at its most acute: 'the shyness is "crippling", it prevents [people] from living the life they want to.' At this end of the spectrum, the shyness may meet the diagnostic criteria for social phobia or social anxiety disorder.

I have experienced this more acute form of shyness, where it crosses into social anxiety disorder, and it was at this stage that I sought professional help. Through cognitive behavioural therapy, I was able to combat the daily panic attacks I suffered in my 20s – more on this later. But perhaps this social anxiety stemmed from my underlying shyness, and that is the personality trait that scientists believe we can control and ultimately change.

That said, both shyness and social anxiety can be circumstantial; emanating fully from a lived experience. So while we may feel confident for long periods, shyness can then be triggered. Dr Erskine remembers a child who was growing up in Africa and had a horrible tooth extraction experience. After that, he became very anxious; he didn't want to go out. He developed social anxiety. 'A child may be perfectly happy but something happens and it makes them want to stay close to their parents,' she says. 'Their confidence can be knocked, leaving them to be fearful. And their response to a traumatic experience may manifest as shyness or social anxiety.'

This nonlinear experience of shyness is documented in the 2017 study that surveyed over 550,000 adults in the UK. Researchers found that although personality is usually considered to be a stable construct, there is evidence to suggest that it in fact changes across the lifespan.[5] They discovered that our personality and propensity towards shyness is affected by our social environment, our parents – particularly our mothers; including their education, interestingly our father's education has no bearing on our levels of shyness – and our income.

In terms of our mothers' education being more impactful on our shyness, this may be associated with the probability that she was primary caregiver to us as children. Educational and child psychologist Hannah Abrahams says that because shy children need to survey, observe and make sense of the world and new situations around them before feeling they can fully participate, 'they often have a greater understanding of social dynamics and networks since they have taken the time to watch'. She explains that children's development is 'very much based on the fine balance of nature and nurture, and children imbibe – and respond to – their parents' examples. So if a child is born to a mother who is quieter, more observational, less socially confident, tenacious or outgoing verbally, a child will often follow their lead.'

But, she says: 'if a child knows and receives the regular emotional validation from their parent, permission to observe and watch, as well as permission and gentle encouragement to participate; they will follow the lead. They will grow in confidence and feel secure to explore their environment and participate with and alongside their peers.' Again, pointing to the notion that shyness isn't fixed.

Abrahams goes on to explain that no child is on a linear trajectory in terms of their development and expression. 'Their life stories and experiences will challenge and support their overall social development and narrative over time. Like with adults, when a child feels safe, secure and cocooned they too will learn to spread their wings as beautifully as we see butterflies do in the summer nights.'

I love this description. And it supports the findings that suggest while we may experience shyness in childhood – that manifests due to our genetic make-up, the conditions we're being raised in, trauma that throws us into some level of social anxiety, or a combination of all three – when we take control over certain parts of our lives, what we earn for example, we are then able to shift away from it. If it feels inhibiting, that is.

Now that I feel fairly confident – in my abilities, but also in social environments – I'm able to reflect on my shyness and see it not as a mental health issue or fault, but as a period I went through, that lasted well into my 20s, and that made me feel sometimes terrified and regularly self-conscious, but also bestowed me with certain attributes. I now feel able to claim it and talk about it and reflect on the ways it helped me to become more empathic and better at listening than I might have been if I had been bolder and more outgoing as a child. I have also retained a fondness for quiet time, and for introspection, which I believe is one of the main reasons I now find myself earning a living from writing.

But something I've found fascinating while researching this book is others' reluctance to admit to their shyness, or to discuss it. I approached people in the public eye who had mentioned their shyness in passing, to garner further information about this, and received curt responses along the lines of: I'm not shy; I may be introverted but definitely not shy. Or they didn't respond at all. And it reminded me of a line in Susan Cain's 2012 book *Quiet: The Power of Introverts in a World That Can't Stop Talking*, where she says, 'Introversion – along with its cousins sensitivity, seriousness and shyness – is now a second-class personality trait, somewhere between a disappointment and a pathology.'

And yet, in the intervening years, we've opened up to introversion. Phrases like JOMO (joy of missing out) to counter the extroverts' FOMO (fear of missing out) mean we are able to make a joke out of being introverted and favouring time alone, rather than being out socialising. But it somehow doesn't feel so funny to explain that you might really *want* to go out but that your shyness is preventing you. I mean, what acronym could we develop for that: SOGO (scared of going out)?

Something else that I noticed happening when I started talking to friends about this book was that everyone had a story to share; about themselves or their child/friend/parent. Some had only just acknowledged, during our conversations, that what they might have experienced in the past was shyness. Like a friend who remembers getting the bus home from school for the first time, aged around 14. As he was approaching his stop, he became incredibly self-conscious about pressing the bell so instead the bus flew right past it. And the next one. And the next one. His shyness had prevented him from alerting the driver that he needed to get off. But it was only as we spoke and he relayed this anecdote that he realised it was shyness that had blocked him. He later worked as a barrister, that's what he was doing when I first met him, so I never would have had him down as a shy person.

But this is what I'm learning: you just never know. I expect many people that I meet now would be surprised to learn that I was so shy, through my childhood and teens. In fact, I think even my friends at that time wouldn't have known, because I hid it so well. That's the thing about shyness: it's all in the mind, so unless you admit to it, people might not always know that it's lurking there. Moreover, as something that isn't necessarily a permanent part of your personality, it might be that you only feel comfortable discussing it if and when it is indeed 'overcome'.

For those who are shy, or have children who are show-ing signs of shyness, these words from psychologist Dr Svanberg may be reassuring:

It's interesting that we have such an aversion to shyness. Like other personality traits, it is something that is very much part of who we are – and has a good evolutionary basis, we can't all be explorers, some of us have to make sure the children are safe! But in a society that values external reward, independence, confidence and individuality, shyness can be seen as an affliction. Generally, if shy people are encouraged to feel safe (whatever this may mean to them), and given time to feel comfortable, they will thrive. Probably the worst thing we can do for a shy person is to push them into situations they don't feel comfortable in – this will raise their anxiety and leave them feeling even less secure. With support, even the shyest children can become more confident about new situations.

The authors of the 2017 Shyness Study came to a similar conclusion, noting that while in most parts of the world today, we value bold and assertive behaviour more highly than shyness or social fear, these evaluations are based on what we presume to be an intrinsic trait, although shyness and confidence will vary across a lifespan. As I mentioned earlier, our feelings and behaviour, in terms of shyness, are affected by employment status, income, education – as well as romantic relationship status (more on that later). And so personality changes over time, which may, they say, 'lend hope to individuals who fear that nothing can be done about their shyness'.

If you are or have been shy, it's not all about trying to escape or hiding this part of your personality or former self. Shyness has its benefits and we'll go on to explore them.

• •

Helen Thorn – stand-up comedian, writer and podcaster, on being shy:

As the fourth child out of five, I was very conscious of finding my place in the family, and at times I was very shy and withdrawn. Being a chubby child growing up in Australia I was self-conscious of my body, as we basically grew up wearing swimmers at all times. So many adults would say unhelpful things like 'Aren't you a BIG GIRL!' which was basically calling me fat and that made me feel very shy. My father was a vicar, so we were constantly surrounded by people in our house and his job was very public, and we were expected to behave in a certain way as vicar's children. But I think that the same thing that made me shy, also motivated me to become a performer. As a child from a large family I had to shout and show off to get attention. And I think I rebelled against being a 'goodie two shoes' vicar's daughter.

My shyness changed over time through discovering my love of school musicals and jazz ballet. Having a sense of humour was a fantastic weapon against shyness. I remember writing a comedy sketch in year five at school camp and everyone laughed. I think that was the first time I did something resembling stand-up and I loved it. There are so many comedians who are actually very shy in real life.

I think when there were situations where I had my body on show, like the swimming pool or ballet classes I felt shy and probably ashamed, too. Growing up in Australia the athletic and slim body were championed and idealised. I felt shy in PE too. I wasn't fast and I wasn't coordinated. I was also bullied a lot growing up. This happened when I moved to a new town when I was nine years old and felt different to the other girls. I became shy and felt like an outsider. Girls can be so cruel at that age, and now that I have a daughter I am so conscious of bullying and her feeling confident.

I have always loved performing. I think it came from my early days in the church choir and school concerts. I grew up in a music-loving family, my mum is always singing and we all learned instruments. I was taken to lots of concerts and shows and watched my mum in amateur dramatics and thought it was so glamourous. Every time there was a school show or musical, I wanted to be part of it. My favourite moment was when I was cast as Björn from ABBA in my school rock and pop through the ages show. I know, the likeness is uncanny.

Now that I am a performer in a double act [Scummy Mummies], I feel so much more confident as I always have my wingman Ellie with me onstage at all times. My greatest fear is not the audience but letting her down and forgetting my lines or saying something that is unfunny. I have had some cruel heckles in the past and that sort of interaction can affect you for a couple of days, because the comments are so personal. But there is nothing better than hearing a whole room laugh at your jokes, so it is always worth the risk – it's the ultimate pay-off.

I am definitely the most confident I have ever been right now. I think I have accepted who I am and love my body. Being a fat person, I have spent so many years of my life feeling shy about how I looked and what others thought of me. But now that I wear a catsuit onstage for my job, I literally have nothing left to hide and that feels liberating. I launched my social media account @helenwearsasize18 to show what a larger body looks like in high street clothes and to champion curvy bodies. So many women have said what I do has helped them with their own shyness and self-confidence and that has meant so much to me. I have also spent the last year training for a marathon, something I never thought I could do as a larger woman. This has changed how I see and value myself and helped me greatly with my confidence.

2

Being shy doesn't make you boring

Everyone is shy – it is the inborn modesty
that makes us able to live in harmony with other
creatures and our fellows. Achievement comes
not by denying shyness but, occasionally,
by setting it aside and letting pride and
perspiration come first.

Kirkpatrick Sale

I mentioned my need, as a child, to always have a best friend. Well, as I got older, I started having relationships, and my boyfriends would become the person I could turn up at events with, confide in and rely on for support. Through my teens and 20s, I was rarely single and at the time I thought I was just having fun. But now I can see that it was more than that; it was about having someone who was always there, in my life, who I could experience new things with. I felt less exposed when I was in a relationship. I felt less shy. And this correlates with evidence that people who aren't in relationships experience the highest levels of shyness.[1] Research has found that people in relationships had consistently lower levels of shyness across the lifespan than people who were not in relationships, and that women who weren't in relationships showed the highest levels of shyness, especially in midlife. Single men were next, and men in relationships had the lowest shyness levels across all age groups.

A reason for this might be that with a partner, we're more likely to have an active social life, which helps us to face – and combat – our social fears. If you have more parties to go to, and someone to go *with*, you are learning how to socialise and in time, may begin to enjoy it. I certainly did. It's like arriving with a form of protection: your partner has your back. Interestingly, research has found that shyness didn't prevent people from entering relationships – clearly it doesn't impact self-esteem enough to make a shy person feel less worthy of having a partner. Or perhaps it's just that when we feel shy, we're willing to work harder to couple up, as we fear aloneness and what that may mean for us socially more than the potential embarrassment of being rejected by someone we are attracted to.

This leads me on to a relationship I had in my early 20s. I'd returned from backpacking around Thailand and India with a friend, and went straight on to Glastonbury Festival. On the last night, I hooked up with a guy I'd hung out with at previous festivals. He was five years older than me and seemed confident. I was young and drunk and quickly fell for him. He seemed to have it all sorted; he was sociable and a charmer. Perhaps I was drawn to him because he seemed so different to me; much like the string of more-confident best friends I'd always had as a child. This makes sense, as a study on personality and mate preferences found that we either find ourselves attracted to people similar to ourselves or who embody what we desire.[2] So I was into him because he had the social confidence I was after. Perhaps I instinctively knew that he would lead me into the personality I wanted to inhabit, whereas hooking up with someone who reinforced my shyness would enhance the likelihood of me continuing to be shy.[3]

And so I went out with this guy for a few years and we were very sociable together. After all, being shy and being unsociable are two altogether different personality dispositions.[4] Clinical neuropsychologist Dr Ruth Erskine explains that some people put a lot of effort into connecting with people. They put themselves out there, even though it's not their inclination. 'But they push themselves because it's important to socialise; to find a way of surviving in a group,' she says. 'Some people are shy but mask it well. And that's different to social anxieties.' That was me: I made an effort to ingratiate myself with people. I often felt like I was desperately treading water when surrounded by this boyfriend's friends – who were all older than me, and at a different stage of their lives – but I managed to keep myself buoyed up because it felt important to learn how to do this.

Dr Eskine also notes that people can be shy in one situation and not in others. She uses the example of starting school, which might be the first time a child is separated from her parents Monday–Friday. 'If we all started school and knew everyone in our class,' she says, 'there might be less incidence of shyness.' Equally, when we feel welcome in an entirely new situation, shyness may not manifest. But if for any reason we feel as if we don't fit in a group – because of age, or any kind of difference – shyness is more likely to arise. That said, there are some people who are naturally inclined to engage more, and others who aren't. So not everyone will enter a room of people they've never met before and retreat into themselves; some will enjoy the challenge and thrive on the opportunity to socialise.

But with me and this boyfriend there was an issue: he didn't have time for quiet people. He found them boring. Somehow, I managed to convince him that I too was confident (probably by mostly being drunk) but after our three-year relationship, a year spent living together, we broke up and his parting words were: you've taught me to be kind; to be more open-minded and accepting of people. Perhaps I'd been waiting for him to see who I really was: a shy, quiet person. And so in preparation for him realising who he'd got into a relationship with, I'd told him to delve beyond the facade. I explained that someone may be quiet but it doesn't mean they're not interesting. I was teaching him this to protect myself, but also because I knew this to be true of other shy people.

Shyness and identity

Elton John's troubled childhood is well documented in the film *Rocketman* and again, in his autobiography *Me*. He describes growing up in the 1950s – 'a very conservative age' – but then Elvis Presley arrived on the scene, John said in a BBC Radio 4 interview, and revolutionised things musically and socially[5] 'and then the 60s happened and all hell broke loose'. Initially, he felt unable to participate. 'I was very shy,' he says. 'I grew up not being able to wear what I wanted to. Winklepicker shoes? No, they were too disgusting. The mods wore chisel toe shoes and anoraks. I couldn't wear those either.'[6] So he changed his name from Reginald Dwight to Elton John, adopted a new persona and lived his 20s in the rebellious way that others might have spent their teens. He became someone new and this gave him the confidence to immerse himself in the music scene he'd been hankering after from a distance.

This tinkering with identity is something I can relate to, having changed my name too – not as dramatically; I went from Anna to Annie; with a brief spell as 'Annie Love', as I played with the idea of pushing my songwriting into a career. But in terms of appearance, I spent my teens moving through various identities – trying out gothic, punk, rocker, skater, *Clueless*-style. These looks were temporary, but I also experimented with piercings and tattoos. It was around the time I met the older boyfriend that I had my first tattoo. Perhaps I wanted to demonstrate how rebellious and bold I was, when really I felt small, scared and uncourageous. I think it mostly worked – if not with him, with my friends. We make snap judgements on a person's entire life, including their personality, within seconds of setting eyes upon them. And my image perhaps gave the impression that I was quite confident.

After separating from my boyfriend, I spent the next few summers working at music festivals, behind the bar. At the time, I had two piercings in my nose, an array of rings down each earlobe, and a couple of tattoos. The people I was working alongside were often similarly tattooed and pierced. At one festival, I was put on a bar with a friend from home and on the second day, she said: 'The other people working with us are so much more open to talking to you than me, because of the way you look.' Until she made this comment, I hadn't given it any thought. Again, I was usually drunk and not paying a huge amount of attention to the nuances of my social interactions. But I started to observe then, and realised she was right: people who were similarly pierced and had different hairstyles (dreadlocks, dyed hair), did seem more open to communicating with me than with my friend.

With hindsight, I can see that I was trying to find a new identity that would free me from the shy, boring person I'd always felt I was. I spoke about this with Laura Fulcher, a child and adolescent psychotherapist, as I was curious to know whether this is common of shy teenagers: experimenting with their appearance. I told her about the time I was hanging out with the 'rockers' at school, and dyed my hair pink. Amongst the group, there was green hair, blue, red, black polka dots. She said: 'And did it work, did it make you feel more confident?' It was only then that I remembered how incredibly self-conscious I felt once I'd washed out the dye and had been left with a head of streaky pink and purple hair. Fortunately, hoodies were part of this particular group's get-up, so I pulled mine over my new hair and hid in it until the dye had washed out a few weeks later.

Fulcher explained that while changing your appearance like this may not have the impact of boosting your confidence, it is generally the children with a more secure base who have the confidence to explore different options. Having been raised by two parents who nurtured, respected and accepted me, I had the confidence to try the punk look – even if I quickly regretted it. But children who have faced more challenges, and don't have that secure attachment with their parents, may be keen to fit in more with the mainstream. They already feel less stable, so they generally don't want to rock the boat further by changing their appearance in a way that will make them stand out more.

There may also be differences between girls and boys in terms of appearance during these formative years. 'Girls are looked at from a really early age and judged for how feminine they are,' says Fulcher. 'This makes them self-conscious. Especially once they're at secondary school; girls seem to then become more critical about their own and other girls' appearances.' She says that most girls, though not all, have fears about their looks and that this is made worse by social media and the online sharing of photos that can be commented on. This objectification of girls, and women, may be partly to blame for more consistent levels of shyness in females, across the lifespan. While boys are taught to be strong and bold and powerful – and place less significance on their looks – girls are told by society that almost all of their worth is tied up with their appearance. Being watched in this way, throughout life, may be a reason for us wanting to withdraw. Moreover, there is an implicit societal insinuation that girls – and women – who speak out are somehow difficult or bolshy, while boys and men who do this are passionate and confident.

Fulcher told me about a client she had, a teenage girl, with bright red hair. She thought the girl looked wonderful but the girl was very shy and self-conscious. There were two issues with the colour of her hair. Firstly, that people with ginger hair are for some reason targeted and openly ridiculed in an incredibly offensive, discriminatory way. And secondly, the colour of her hair made her different. She wanted to fit in and be like the others, but felt the colour of her hair prevented this.

I wondered how Fulcher works with adolescents who are suffering with identity issues and she said that she tries to help them to get a sense of themselves, which can be achieved through creativity. In her practice, she uses paint and clay, and encourages her patients to get creative with words, ideas. 'It's about trying to listen to them so they can build a picture of themselves that has values and talent. It's slow work.' She also asks them to create a 'soul picture', which is a visual representation of themselves, often made using collage. 'It's about thinking about who you are and feeling that is OK,' she explains.

This feeling of wanting to fit in is familiar to singer, songwriter, producer and actress Beyoncé Knowles. In an interview with Oprah Winfrey, when Oprah asks if she was always the prettiest girl in her class, Beyoncé responds: 'No, I was very shy and a little awkward . . . I had really big ears that I cover up right now [she says this while pulling her hair over her ears] . . . and I was chubby. I had my time; I was really shy.' She remembers kids making fun of her ears, holding up pillows on each side of their faces, pretending to be Beyoncé.

Later, Beyoncé created an alter ego called Sasha Fierce to help her combat feelings of shyness before performing. In another interview, Oprah asks about at what stage Sasha Fierce shows up, when Beyoncé is preparing for a show.[7] Beyoncé replies: 'Usually when I hear the crowd, when I put on my stilettos. The moment right before, when you're nervous and that other thing kind of takes over for you. Then Sasha Fierce appears and my posture and the way I speak – and everything – is different.' She goes on to compare a stage show to acting: 'When you put on the wig, put on the clothes, you walk different . . . it's kind of this character I've created over the years.'

So if Beyoncé is still using an alter ego to help her manage her shyness – well, that certainly makes me feel a lot better.

3

You *can* ~~always~~ get what you want (without being loud)

There was a whole magnificent
soul burning brightly behind her 'shy'.

Atticus

When I was four or five, my parents bought me a bike for my birthday. My dad put stabilisers on it. After a few days, I asked him to remove them. He wasn't sure that was a good idea but didn't want to temper my spirits so he gently asked if I was sure I was ready, as he thought it might be worth practising for a while longer. But I repeated my request. He took the stabilisers off and I rode straight up the garden on my own. I remember how it felt. Perhaps I'd spent some time watching my older sister ride her bike and some of my friends, who were all a bit older than me as I had a birthday later in the academic year, and I felt behind. Or maybe I just knew it would feel fun to cycle. But I had a strong need to ride a bike properly – and right at that moment. I didn't want to wait.

My dad told that story at my wedding, as an example of my willpower and determination when I've set my sights on something. Like my husband. Though fortunately the feelings were mutual, so in that instance it wasn't so much about the powers of my persuasion and more about a joint decision. My dad said: 'Annie always manages to get what she wants.' But that's not entirely true, because if there's an element of competition involved, if I want what someone else also wants, I duck out. I won't battle it out. But when the challenge is singular to me, it's about achieving something at no one else's expense, I do have a fair amount of determination.

I was never adventurous as a child, though, and never the first to do something. I'm still never the first. I hang back, observe, and then – if I decide it's something I might enjoy or gain from doing – I give it a shot. It has always had to be in my own time, though. I remember around a similar time to the bike-riding incident, going to a playground with my reception class. The teacher told me to try the monkey bars; the other kids were trying them. But I didn't want to and knew I wouldn't be able to. I tried to explain this to her – after all, I was bigger than most of the other kids; heavier – but she wasn't interested. And I wasn't loud enough. So she kept cajoling and eventually, I caved in. I reached for the first bar, grabbed it tightly, then attempted to swing my body so that I could reach for the second bar with my other hand, but as suspected, I wasn't strong enough. I fell to the ground and landed on my back. I can't remember if an ambulance was called, I think one probably was, but I can still see the look on my teacher's face: pure panic.

As the parent, carer or teacher of a shy child, it can be a challenge determining when you should encourage the child to participate and when you should go easy; really listen to their reservations. Richard Branson tells an interesting story about his mother's attempt to rid him of his shyness.[1] Apparently she was concerned that if he continued to be introverted and shy, it would hold him back in later life so she continuously challenged him. 'She tried to drum it out of me by explaining that shyness is a form of selfishness,' he says. 'She'd tell me that being shy was merely thinking of oneself, rather than wanting to make other people happy.'

One of her methods of shyness exorcism was to encourage him and his sisters to perform at the dinner parties she held, which would be a real challenge for many shy children. But there was another quite shocking attempt to 'cure' him, too. When he was about six years old, she decided that his shyness was now utterly unacceptable. So after a shopping trip in town, she pulled the car over to the side of the road, about three miles from their home, and told him to get out and walk. Her thinking was that the only way he'd achieve this was by asking adults for directions. He remembers it taking a lot longer than she'd anticipated – 'she had not accounted for time to stop to look at bugs and inspect rocks' – but he did make it home. And after that, he felt more confident about talking to grown-ups and expressing himself.

Branson goes on to say that he wouldn't recommend this approach, necessarily, but believes that it taught him what he considers to be life's greatest lesson: 'growth happens when you put yourself outside your comfort zone'. And so, while even now he feels shy from time to time, he also continues to throw himself into situations that force him to tackle his fears head-on. He says he is eternally grateful to his mother, as this approach to challenges paved the way for an exciting life and career.

Branson's business success is a great example of the fact that you don't need to be a naturally outgoing person to succeed. And in fact, I wonder if facing the challenge of shyness as a child – particularly when you have parents or teachers who tell you it's not OK and that it needs to be 'fixed' – might instil a certain resolve. Each day can feel like a mini challenge when just walking into school fills you with slight dread. And when you're being told to get up and perform, to snap out of it, you're forced to adopt a new persona. Your own version of Sasha Fierce. But what you retain is a sharp memory of how it feels to be the quiet one and so you can use this when you then spot shyness in others. There's more on shyness and leadership in chapter five.

Shyness doesn't mean you can't be adventurous

In my late teens, after finishing my A levels, I worked for six months, then stuffed a backpack with impractical shoes, clothes and way too many hardback books (eight, I believe) and headed to Asia with my best friend, Lizzie. We'd planned a six-month trip around Thailand and India – a 'gap year', if you like. I don't remember feeling nervous; after all, I wasn't going alone – I had a companion. But my parents were nervous for me. They didn't try to stop me, having spent their late teens travelling the world together. And being a self-interested teenager meant it never occurred to me that they might be worried about me going. But they were.

As I said, I'd never been the adventurous child; that was my sister. She was the one who made friends wherever she went, tried out new activities, went camping for weeks and never seemed to miss home. I was the one who stayed closer to home, didn't want to go to university, and probably looked like I might never stray too far.

However, I have an adventurous and spontaneous streak; I enjoy new experiences – and I enjoy challenging people's perception of me. So I planned that six-month trip with Lizzie, then waved goodbye to my parents at the airport, and jetted off to freedom. My dad told a friend, while I was away on that trip, that he was looking forward to getting to know me all over again once I returned. I think what he meant was: this trip is going to change her, and I think it will be a good thing. I'm not suggesting my dad thought there was anything wrong with me; he didn't. But he knew that pushing myself out of my comfort zone like that would be good for me.

And he was right: I was different when I returned. Braver and more confident. I agreed to work at the Edinburgh Festival on a play with a load of people I'd never met. I went to Paris on my own. I started throwing myself into new and exciting opportunities because I knew now that I could do it. These new experiences put me in varying degrees of danger and discomfort. I had to navigate different languages and cultures. But after each trip, I returned feeling a little less shy and a lot more capable.

A 2013 study on temperament and personality found that our personality is initially shaped by how we react physiologically to various life experiences.[2] We then develop our own personal goals for who we want to be and what we want to achieve, and our personality becomes self-regulated, to some degree, as we adapt to higher standards. We use past experiences to teach us how to move forward in life, so when we force ourselves to face a fear and discover that actually we are able to do that thing that we felt physically unable to do previously – for instance, travel abroad alone – this in part moulds our personality. We become braver in character.

Actress Michelle Dockery, who rose to fame as the rather cold Lady Mary Crawley in the period TV drama *Downton Abbey*, initially found it difficult being in the spotlight, as she suffered with shyness. She was keen to act, but not to do the red carpet stuff, or any of the other PR activities that are now seen as an intrinsic part of an actor's job. 'Initially I would get really nervous,' she said in an interview with the *Independent*, 'I can be quite shy and I didn't want to do anything except the acting. I found talking about myself especially difficult. But you learn that you don't have to talk about your private life; you don't have to please everyone.'[3] She learned to accept this uncomfortable aspect of her acting career, and came to realise 'that stuff can be fun if you embrace it all'. She chose to adapt her mindset and in doing so, the shyness began to disappear.

There is no greater example of being able to get what you want – without being a naturally outgoing person – than that of civil rights campaigner Rosa Parks refusing, in 1955, aged 42, to give up her seat on the public bus for a white person. She'd experienced racial discrimination her whole life and on that one day, decided she'd had enough. She chose to break the law because people of colour had been repressed and mistreated for far too long, and this single act of bravery began the Montgomery Bus Boycott, which led to nationwide efforts to end racial segregation of public facilities. And yet Rosa Parks was known to be 'shy and quiet-spoken'.[4] It's sometimes our actions and determination that matter more than the volume of our voice.

• •

DJ Nikki Beatnik, who tours the world, dj-ing with Kelis, shares her experience of shyness:

I was quite a chilled kid who loved music from an early age, reading, animals and art. I grew up in a remote part of the Scottish Highlands until I was ten, I only had six kids in my entire school, so I was around my immediate family and adult friends most of the time. I got a place at music school when I was seven, which took me to a city every weekend and I met different people but I was never a pushy or loud kid.

When we moved to England, I went from a school with six people to 1,000 pupils. I was very good at cello but I remember getting onstage to sing or play in front of strangers and it being very daunting, and shyness would kick in to the point where I would worry, but maybe it was because I had dealt with a lot of changes socially. I probably compensated by being funny and trying to fit in and if that didn't work and I got bullied for my accent or playing classical music or just being different – I would end up fighting.

I knew I was pretty talented at classical music and playing orchestra from an early age but no one else in my family had a job in the creative fields despite all being creative so there was no talk of being a professional musician at school or at home. It didn't seem a reality. As a teenager I fell in love with club culture, hip hop and house music, and raving and I switched my attention to dj-ing from around fifteen or sixteen. This was around 1989–90, and there were hardly any women dj-ing and it was extremely daunting to even try to compete. In clubs, it felt like all eyes were on you; waiting for you to mess up. And it was a very male-dominated culture compared to now, so again the same feelings I'd had when performing classical music – and having to deal with the fact that I desperately wanted to perform but also hated performing and being stared at by people – arose again. It was a real dichotomy. The first time I played in a club my hands were shaking so much I couldn't lift the needle on the record. It's a stressful situation, for sure.

It's a really weird thing to just stand in front of people that are waiting to be entertained and impressed and to then do your thing perfectly – even then they may not like you because you are too young, too female, too old, too fat, too thin, wrong hair. There are so many reasons, once you realise people can just dislike you for pretty much nothing and you stick two fingers up to that and do it anyway, the whole world is an easier place. You also realise you might not always get it right or be flawless but that's what makes you an interesting performer and having the balls and charisma to do it and appear fearless, even if inside you are crapping yourself, is the main stumbling block of why people hold themselves back.

As you get older you realise that pushing yourself through that fear is a tool and usually leads to better things and you really can't control what other people think of you, so just do it. Don't get stuck in your own head. I realised that quite young. I'm still quite an introverted person who prefers my own company, but I can dress up and show up and handle meetings and get onstage at Glastonbury or anywhere around the world and not feel scared or intimidated. It's a learning curve.

In terms of being physically able to do it, the main thing is 10,000+ hours of practice so that you are very confident in your skills as a musician, but in terms of actually booking gigs and getting contacts etc., that's a lifetime of business knowledge and hustle and with each gig you get better and more confident. There was quite a gap between learning at fifteen or sixteen and then really making a go of it in clubs and dj-ing. Some of that was down to fewer opportunities for women, it was a much tougher scene with less visibility and hard to break through and get taken seriously. Some of the time I was studying for a degree and then needed a proper job to pay the bills (I went into advertising first).

I had been running my own raves all through college, so I gained experience there. The thing that really pushed me the hardest was doing jobs I hated. Working for other people, so I literally forced myself to do the most crazy things outside my comfort zone, that made me feel so sick to the stomach, and then I thought to myself: 'If you can do that, you can get up and dj in front of people.' Long story short, I started running my own club nights in London. And it grew from there. I look back and every gig I've done from a child to now has been one big learning curve and confidence-builder.

That said, even now I'm not that comfortable in new groups of people or if I go to an event on my own or have to speak in front of a lot of people. But I forced myself to do a lot of panels recently so I'm getting more blasé about it. Weirdly I can go to a club or festival on my own and not feel shy at all, so it's definitely practice.

I should note that most people would say that I am in no way shy. They would say I am a very confident person, feisty and bossy at times, but this has probably been a learned behaviour in response to many life experiences where I would have been and have been trampled all over if I didn't become able to speak up for myself.

Now I am always the one who speaks up in most situations regardless of what others think and I've learned to because I've had to fight for everything career-wise from a child to now. I think a lot of musicians and artists I know have probably been the same and the face you see onstage is slightly different to them in real life. It takes a lot to be able to deal with the constant rejection, highs and lows and judgement in the creative arts for a start. So probably yes, celebrities, or maybe more accurately artists, can be shy and sometimes life has a way of kicking these types of personalities down as being not as valid as the loud confident people. So I would say they probably made a conscious decision at some point that doing what they loved and getting onstage was more important than self-doubt and being shy.

There is absolutely nothing wrong with being shy or quieter than others. Some of the best musicians, producers and artists are introverts. Sometimes being quiet and observing can get you a lot of insight.

4

Quiet people are more introspective

I was passionate. I found something that I loved. I could be all alone in a big old skating rink and nobody could get near me and I didn't have to talk to anybody because of my shyness. It was great. I was in my fantasy world.

Dorothy Hamill

When I was about sixteen, I travelled to Newcastle on the train to see my older sister, as she was at university up there. I bought myself a new outfit – knee-length denim skirt, light brown woollen jumper and dark brown knee-high flat boots – and felt good: confident, independent. She met me at the train station and we travelled to her halls of residence, where she introduced me to her roommates. I probably didn't say very much but then as excited freshers, most of them rabbited on regardless, so it went unnoticed.

We went out that night to the student union bar and drank a drink called Skittles, a mix of various alcoholic drinks and juices that created a colourful, sweet and – crucially – strong drink. We got drunk. I felt my inhibitions slip away and laughed and danced and chatted with all these older people in this new environment. But while the night was fun, the next day wasn't so much. Being hungover made me feel even more acutely aware of myself. So when we met one of my sister's friends for lunch, I sat, ate and didn't say very much. It wasn't that I found the conversation boring – I didn't – but I just couldn't think of anything to contribute.

After lunch, when my sister and I headed back to the train station – without the friend – she said: 'Do you know that you were silent that entire lunch?' She wasn't being rude or mean, she was genuinely curious. I probably shrugged and mumbled something about being hungover, but what someone who isn't shy might not understand about those who are is this: you are *always* aware of how little you have said. I would have spent that entire lunch trying to think of something to say – but failing. You are acutely aware of everything you are doing that isn't what is socially expected of you.

I now wonder if perhaps I was able to be silent that day because my sister was there to do the talking. As children, she might have sometimes acted as my mouthpiece, in the same way that my eldest child talks for her younger brother. She has the words that he can't always conjure, so she does him a favour and says out loud what it is that she knows he's trying to say. It's quite impressive how well an older child can decipher the language of their younger sibling in a way that sometimes eludes grown-ups. But this can then make the younger child reliant on the older one to communicate his or her thoughts. Growing up, my sister was the more outgoing child. She didn't seem fazed by attention. And that day, while we ate lunch in Newcastle, perhaps I felt protected by my older sister and thought: she can do the talking while I sit back and observe.

But whether it's based partly in sibling relationships or not, a shy adult will never be opting out of conversation in a social setting without an acute awareness of herself. This is why I defy anyone who suggests shyness doesn't make you more introspective. When you sit through a meal out in public and you don't talk, what could you possibly be doing if not thinking about yourself and your behaviour?

According to an article on *Verywell Mind* by Kendra Cherry, MS – author and educational consultant who teaches psychology – there are two types of introspection in psychology; one is about general, day-to-day introspection, while the other is a formal research technique that was first developed by psychologist Wilhelm Wundt.[1] Focusing on the more casual form of introspection, Cherry writes,

> 'Introspection as reflection . . . involves informally examining our own internal thoughts and feelings. When we reflect on our thoughts, emotions, and memories and examine what they mean, we are engaged in introspection.'

For me, a quiet lunch – or turning up at any social event and not having much to say – means that I become very introspective; I examine my reason for not interacting. I observe what it is about some people that brings me out of myself while others make me withdraw. I focus solely on my thoughts and feelings, because that's all I have when no words are coming out of my mouth. I believe it's helped me to understand myself – and others – better. After all, hour upon hour spent listening in, analysing other people's words, behaviour and confidence is sure to instil some wisdom on human nature.

From a young age, I began channelling this into my writing: notes, poetry, articles, blog posts. I discovered that while I couldn't always articulate my thoughts on the world and its inhabitants verbally, I could usually get it down on paper. This is why it doesn't surprise me to learn that there are so many writers, artists, thinkers and creatives who identify as shy. And it does bring reassurance, as these are some incredibly successful people.

Radiohead frontman Thom Yorke is known for his intense, emotive songwriting. His lyrics are impassioned and reflective. In an interview for *Crack Magazine* – when asked about the 'creative burst' that led to him recording a new solo record, writing his first piece of classical music and scoring a film soundtrack – he described spending a lot of time in his basement studio, over a two-year period, 'and suddenly everything that was kicking around in [my head] is starting to come out,' he said. Yorke, in fact, becomes so introspectively engaged with his imagination that when he revisits music he's made, it's unfamiliar. 'Sometimes I don't even recognise myself in some of the music I made,' he said, 'which is always what I'm looking for, I guess.'[2]

In the same interview, he's asked about the dystopian feel to the single he's just released and, in his answer, Yorke remembers a jet-lagged night in Tokyo. 'There was one night where I'd go to sleep, two hours later I'm absolutely wide awake and I just had these images . . . humans and rats changed places. A dream. And as I came out, I woke up with this really strong set of images of girls in tottering heels, but they're actually rats, and the human beings are in the drains. I had another one, these weird images of the City of London, and all the skyscrapers are just shuffling along.' And it was this image that inspired the record. He wanted to find a way to illustrate a feeling of anxiety in his music, and found this could be achieved through dystopian imagery.

The need to express his inner world through his music is in no way singular to Yorke. In fact, what songwriting *isn't* about ordering the writer's thoughts on an issue or emotion through lyrics? It's just that Yorke's approach; revealing so much in his songs, suggests he relies heavily on this outlet. Interestingly, in a Vimeo video called 'Ask a Grown Man',[3] Yorke responds to the question: 'How do you tell the boy you have a crush on that you have a crush on him if you are really, really, really shy?' by suggesting putting pen to paper instead: 'If you have a crush on him, if you're really, really, really, really shy, which is what I was at that age – also, I was at a boys' school so it was impossible to meet girls anyway – how about just write him a note, if you can't bear to talk to him,' says Yorke. Again, using the written word to convey the strong emotions you're feeling inside.

Illustrator Stacie Swift has an interesting take on how her shyness affected her creative career. 'I think my shyness was largely a by-product of low self-confidence,' she says. 'I'd step back from putting myself in the spotlight in any way, didn't attempt things that I felt I didn't have a natural aptitude for and would generally avoid any situations that were out of my comfort zone.' She wonders if having a more extroverted personality might have helped when she started an all-girls' secondary. Later, she did become more confident and less shy, but she can still see both advantages and disadvantages to shyness. On the one hand, she says: 'Shyness meant I was always very much an observer – so able to read social situations and emotions well, which has proved a useful skill to have, especially in a career that relies on communicating ideas and creating work that is relatable, and invokes an emotional reaction.' On the other hand, she says that while she loves solitude, which is useful as a freelance illustrator: 'It would likely have been more difficult to have succeeded in this field had I remained as shy as I was – there is a lot of need to self-promote, negotiate, protect your work, etc., that doesn't go hand-in-hand with being timid.'

In terms of introspection, Swift says she's always been an 'over-thinker' and quite emotionally driven. 'From when I was little I used writing – often poetry – and art as a way to reflect and process thoughts and feelings.' She thinks having the ability to be acutely reflective and analytical – 'both of yourself and the world around you' – feeds into creating work that resonates with a wide audience.

She still feels shy sometimes, for instance when entering a crowd of people she's never met before, and dislikes phone conversations and video calls with strangers. 'If I'm feeling low or tired, etc., for any reason, I'm naturally inclined to return into my shell for a bit and hide away,' she says. But she had to overcome her shyness when there was upheaval and a change in family dynamics during her teenage years. 'It definitely served as a catalyst for me becoming more self-assured – and to a certain degree, there was no other option except to find my voice and use it – a blessing very much in disguise, as life has progressed.' But while she recognises that the self-promotion element of her job is not easy work for a shy person, she doesn't dismiss shyness as being a negative trait: 'I don't think shyness is necessarily a bad thing,' she says. 'The quiet reflection and introversion can be a great source for creativity. Plus, being highly attuned to your own thoughts and emotions is a positive – it can be useful being very aware of yourself and how things affect and impact you.'

5

Shyness can help with your career

Part of why I started a band was due
to feelings of shyness and social ineptitude.
I saw it as some way of being able to interact
with people from a safe distance.

Jarvis Cocker

When I left home for university, I felt as if I was now living as an independent adult. I had to look after myself and make big decisions. But really, it was entering the world of work that made me realise it was all down to me. No student loan, no three-year study period to focus on – just me, a plan to be a professional writer and a long future ahead of me. After completing a BA in English at Sussex University, I returned to London, moved back in with my parents and applied for every job going, before settling on interning at national newspapers and broadcasters, while working nights on the door of a nightclub in Camden.

During an internship at ITN, researching for the More4 news show, Krishnan Guru-Murthy invited me for lunch with him and a group of other newsreaders. We went to a basement restaurant and sat on stools around a high table. I was about twenty-three, desperate to break into journalism and was sitting with these intelligent, influential journalists. If I'd joined in their conversations about current affairs – I knew what they were talking about, I had opinions – I might have secured myself a paid position. But I didn't because I was too shy.

There was also the time I was interning at the *Western Gazette* newspaper in Somerset, where I moved after studying for a journalism MA in London, and I was writing dozens of articles each week. I'd been there a couple of months, unpaid, and the office manager, who dabbled in recruitment, told me there was someone new joining the team as a junior reporter. I was working as a junior reporter – going out into the community, conducting interviews, writing up news stories – they just weren't paying me. It turned out this guy had been living near me in Hackney, east London, and while I'd moved to Somerset to live with my boyfriend, he had moved just for the job. There was nothing rooting him to Yeovil. I was already living there, working for the newspaper. I had all the qualifications required; he would need to be taught shorthand on the job. And yet they hired him over me.

A few months later, I couldn't afford to stay on unpaid. I told them I was leaving and the office manager looked a bit confused; perhaps she thought I'd continue working for free for a few years. Perhaps she felt guilty about how she'd treated me. Either way, other reporters were commenting on how much I'd contributed and said they were dismayed by me not being hired. One suggested I book a meeting with the new female editor of the newspaper. I'd had chats with her, and she seemed open and friendly. I reckon if I'd made that meeting with her, explained how much work I'd done and pitched for a job, she'd have made it happen. My mother-in-law tried to encourage me to ask for the meeting too, making suggestions for what I could say. But I didn't do it. I felt too shy.

There were many more incidences of my shyness preventing me from succeeding with my career but, while it took me time to get to where I wanted to be – a successful freelance journalist was always *the dream* – there was something going on under the surface that was indeed propelling me forward. That same quiet determination that made me ask my dad to remove my stabilisers so that I could ride up the garden on my bike made me closely observe what employers valued in their employees. I noted the importance of punctuality, hard work, innovation and politeness. These were all characteristics I'd picked up off the back of shyness (being scared to be late, fear of failure, quietly mulling over ideas, never wanting to offend). And over the years, I developed good relationships with the people I worked for and the editors who commissioned me. In time, I was being contacted by the *Guardian* – rather than endlessly pitching to them – to write articles. My quiet perseverance and hard work had paid off.

After working as a freelance journalist for a few years, as well as launching my own parenting and lifestyle platform *The Early Hour*, and having my first book published, I decided to launch an online course. I'd heard it was a good way to create a passive income stream and – pregnant with my third baby and still freelance, so not entitled to any maternity leave and only pitiful maternity allowance from the Government – this appealed. I created a course teaching freelancers and business owners how to do their own PR, and it sold out in two days. I'd secured £3,000 in two days. I ran the course and launched another one, teaching women how to become their own boss, and it was similarly successful. Soon, I was earning £10,000 a month from these courses; enough for my husband to quit his job to help me grow the business and look after our young children.

I'm now running The Robora – our online course business – and employing a handful of freelancers for ad hoc work. Going from shy child to boss of a business feels unlikely, until it happens. But now I can see that my shyness has helped me to make this happen. I've quietly squirrelled away, growing my online platform and audience so that I have people to sell to. I tried various businesses before this:

selling jumpsuits I imported from India, restoring retro furniture, selling second-hand clothes on eBay, for example. Being shy doesn't mean not having gusto, and it doesn't mean being unable to succeed in business. I just needed to find the right idea and, once I had, I could channel all my energy into it. Now, I run the business by listening to my customers and online community, and making changes according to what they want and need.

A 2016 study on 'leading with introversion' found some common advantages to being shy, or introverted, in the workplace (these terms are used interchangeably throughout the study).[1] They are as follows:

- Monitoring self and other.

- Refraining from action.

- Observing at a distance.

- Listening as a way of being present. Many participants describe being astute listeners, and how the receptive and appreciative states give them critically important information.

- Sitting with silence.

- Perspective-taking.

These attributes were amassed following interviews with introverted people. However, the advantages of a quieter leader are also documented in a 2012 study by Beukeboom, Tanis, and Vermeulen.[2] While they concluded that extroverts tend to be perceived as more personally engaged and conversational, they also found that introverts' slower, more careful approach to language tended to increase the level of trustworthiness perceived by listeners. And in business, trust matters. Hugely. And so while we'd mostly imagine extroverts – more outwardly confident people – to make better bosses, that's not always the case.

Two experiments were carried out for a Harvard Business Review study, to determine whether sometimes a shy or more introverted boss might have a more positive impact on employees.[3] After all, a shy worker may feel too intimidated by a loud, outgoing employer to offer ideas and innovate. In this study – 'The Hidden Advantages of Quiet Bosses' – questionnaires were sent out to managers and employees at 130 franchises of a US pizza delivery company. The bosses were asked how extroverted they considered themselves to be, and the employees were asked how often they and their colleagues tried to suggest new ways of doing things in the business. The results showed that in shops where employees were less proactive, extroverted leadership was associated with 16 per cent higher profits than average. But in franchises where workers offered ideas, extroverted leadership was associated with 14 per cent lower profits than with an introverted boss, suggesting that for teamwork – employer and employees working together to boost sales – the quieter bosses come up trumps.

There was another experiment: 163 college students were asked to work in groups to see how many T-shirts they could fold in ten minutes. Within these groups, there was one leader and four followers, two of whom were undercover research assistants, in on the experiment. To manipulate the leaders, they each read a statement before the activity began – some were statements by extroverted leaders (like JFK and Martin Luther King, Jr.), while others read a statement praising reserved leaders (like Gandhi and Abraham Lincoln). Some followers were also given impetus to encourage them to be more proactive followers – like the undercover research assistants stopping them and suggesting a better way to do the task. The groups with an introverted leader and proactive followers folded, on average, 28 per cent more T-shirts. They found the extroverted leaders were more threatened by and unreceptive to proactive employees. The introverted leaders listened carefully and made employees feel valued, which motivated them to work hard.

Again, this shows the introverted leaders being more open to teamwork, which creates a more harmonious workplace.

Maybe this is one of the reasons Marissa Mayer, former CEO of Yahoo, was believed to have changed the internal culture at Yahoo for the better. She was one of Google's first twenty employees, and moved up through the ranks to a leadership position there before transferring over to Yahoo. On a side note, she briefly dated Google co-founder Larry Page and their dalliance was described by a colleague as 'Two quiet people dating each other quietly.' So she was clearly perceived by co-workers as shy.

At the time of her move to Yahoo, the company was plummeting and during her five-year tenure she managed to more than triple the value of the shares. But in the end, Yahoo couldn't keep up with its competitors – Facebook and Google – and was bought out by Verizon, which is when Mayer left. During her time at Google and Yahoo, she started mentoring schemes and brought in management coaches, to empower employees. She said: 'Really in technology, it's about the people, getting the best people, retaining them, nurturing a creative environment and helping to find a way to innovate.'[4] Her words and her work are testament to the empathy that might be more commonly attributed to a shy leader.

Louise McKee, former HR director for both Tesco and Barclays Bank, and now an executive coach, took a different approach to her work. As one of the few women in a senior role at these companies in the 90s, she felt obliged to fake extraversion in order to get ahead. She was born in Northern Ireland, one of six children, and remembers big family get-togethers where she'd help her mum lay out the food; she'd do her bit, then retreat to the bedroom and curl up in her bunk bed 'hoping no one would see me so I could read'. Her mother would come and find her, telling her to say hello to relatives and once again, she'd join the fray. 'I liked the noise,' she says, 'I still like the company of noise; I have the radio on in the background if I'm working, but I didn't always want to participate.'

However, she could see that it was important to speak out sometimes so by observing other kids in the playground – 'I remember watching and assessing,' she says – Mckee learned about extrovert behaviour that she could adopt when she needed to. 'I held my own counsel,' she says. 'I had the confidence to speak out. But people would have said I was shy, as I was harder to get at than some of my siblings.' She's quick to point out that it didn't mean she didn't have a view, but this quietness and tendency to withdraw a little meant she became a good listener. 'I learned through listening and watching,' she says. 'Some of my siblings learned by doing; putting themselves out there.'

McKee moved to London and worked as a secretary before embarking on a career in the corporate world, making her way up to a senior position at Tesco. It was at this stage that she realised 'business leaders need to be extroverted or to fake it'. Knowing that she wasn't a natural extrovert, she started studying psychometrics. She did a masters in organisational psychology. She realised that the better she knew herself and her personality type, the more equipped she would be to put forward ideas in meetings.

'Being quiet about a really good idea when you're employed to have them isn't going to work,' she says. 'If you have ideas for how to improve the business, or a service – you must not be quiet.' She feels that men are more overtly competitive in business 'and you quickly learn that if you don't meet them on some level, you'll get sidelined or steamrolled'. McKee had one experience where a man she was reporting to wasn't good at his job. Over time, she grew tired of feeling as if she should be in his job position and decided that she'd rather leave the business than work under him. It was at this point that she utilised what she'd learned from being a quiet child; observing, assessing – as well as her psychometrics studies – to get what she wanted from the situation. Rather than bowling in and demanding he quit, or threatening that she would leave, she arranged meetings, carefully communicating her unease about him. The guy was asked to leave and she was promoted to his position.

'It's about learning who you are and about how to handle yourself in the world,' says McKee. 'I'd recommend young women coming up behind me – who face the same challenges, working in a male-dominated environment – to do psychometrics, find out your personality type. And learn how to use other behaviours.' She says that her shyness, or introversion, gave her the ability to analyse people's behaviours. 'Where others rushed in and made a fool of themselves, I'd learned a lot from being in a big family, and wanting to belong, about the importance of holding back.' She says that while shy people and introverts tend to have very clear thoughts and views, because they've had time to consider them, they then need to employ extrovert behaviours to get their ideas across. 'We've got to be able to say: here's my good work, and to have that respected and accepted. Otherwise no one promotes us.'

This resonates with me; a feeling of inner quietness at odds with the need to raise my voice in order to be heard. Having sat through many a class, seminar, lecture and meeting desperate to say something but not sure if my contribution would be of any value, I came up with a technique for ensuring I contributed everything I wanted to say, without fluffing my words. I started writing notes. I'd take my notebook into job interviews, I'd have it open during classes, I would also take it with me on the stage for any panel talks I was part of – I still do. There is always a fear that once you put your hand up, or start your sentence – and all eyes are on you – you'll mess it up and ruin your moment in the spotlight. A notebook became my method for ensuring this wouldn't happen. I've had employers laugh at me, kindly, in interviews, and audience members do the same during talks when I've pulled it out to remind myself of a book or app I want to recommend. But I realised, over time, that it's OK to be human; to be flawed. Not only am I shy, but I also have a terrible memory, so my notebook-wherever-I-go is doubly advantageous.

Apparently Richard Branson is also a fan of a notebook. Being at the helm, he is taking a different stance, though, which is that to be a good leader, you must always be paying attention to what your employees are telling you. 'As a leader, you should always be listening,' he said. 'Be visible, note down what you hear and you'll be surprised how much you learn. Successes happen from working and learning with some of the world's most inspiring and inspired people.'[5] This desire to listen and learn may well come from Branson's own shyness. He is able to sit back, be quiet, listen, reflect in a way that a more confident or out-going leader can't. When a boss is able to respect his juniors and to make them feel heard, there is better staff retention but also less space for conflict. Being able to speak up when there's an issue is important for a harmonious workplace. It can feel incredibly daunting to vocalise a workplace issue, even for someone confident. But for a shy person, it's even harder. However, in the same way that McKee said we must ensure we don't shy away from promoting ourselves and the work we're producing, there might also be negative work situations we find ourselves in that require a loud voice to combat.

I once worked in a role where I was managing an art and music space, and had to report to a board of trustees. On the whole, I got on very well with them, but there was one female among a group of males, and she had a very clear vision for how the space should be used. That in itself wasn't a bad thing; she was a strong, intelligent leader. But it was the way she delivered her ideas that I sometimes found difficult, because it felt like there was no space for my voice.

However, there was this one day when she'd been watching over me all morning as I worked, questioning everything I was doing. I had been working so hard, as I always did – and the work was paying off – but she was hovering because of her own boredom or need to exercise some power over me, and I snapped. She'd grilled me one too many times and I turned and said: 'Why are you standing there criticising me? I work hard and I don't deserve this scrutiny.' She was shocked. And silenced. She retreated and later emailed, apologising for her behaviour. After that, the playing field levelled out. Perhaps she developed some respect for me, for standing up for myself. Maybe she'd spent a long time trying to prove herself in a male-dominated environment and had forgotten that not everyone is a threat. Whatever it was, I learned that day that while being hard-working, flexible and compliant is important as an employee, so is finding your voice when someone is taking the piss.

I think it might be common amongst shy people to put up with a certain amount of piss-taking before it builds up too much and eventually, you burst. Perhaps we have the advantage, in the workplace, of being able to hold our tongue when necessary to avoid conflict. But equally, our employers and colleagues have the disadvantage of seeing us whip up into a fury when they push us too far. That trustee wasn't the only employer I've had who has taken advantage of my quiet nature to the point that it's simply not acceptable and I tell them where to stick it.

There was another situation at a tech company I was working for, as a copywriter. I had to liaise regularly with the social media manager – send him copy to approve before it was scheduled to go out. And over a period of a few weeks, he stopped responding to my emails. So I'd work hard on the copy, send it over and then . . . nothing. I let it go the first few times, assuming he was really busy, but it might be important to note that he wasn't my senior; we were equal within the hierarchy of the company. He then started to be negative about the copy I was sending; unnecessarily so. Picking the tiniest fault. After a few weeks, I'd had enough. It was preventing me from doing my job properly, all the negativity and lack of response, so I went over to his desk first thing one morning and asked to have a word with him outside. He looked shocked, and scared. I explained that I was finding it frustrating that he wasn't replying to my emails and that when we eventually did meet to talk about the copy, he never had anything positive to say. He was very apologetic, and said he hadn't meant it. After that, he replied to my emails and only shared criticism when necessary.

As McKee said above: the quieter people analyse situations. So while the more outgoing members of staff are floating about, behaving however they like; without thinking about how others might feel, we are noticing this and ordering our thoughts. By the time we've had enough, we know exactly what we're going to say and how we're going to say it, because we've been going over it time and time again in our heads. So we can then deliver an eloquent explanation about why something isn't working, which leaves our colleagues – like that social media guy – clambering for words and excuses and explanations. In conclusion, don't underestimate the strength of a shy person who feels undermined.

In general, it can be easy for employers and co-workers to misjudge a shy person as someone who has less ambition and drive, and less to contribute. But it's worth breaking through the quiet facade to see what's going on inside. If you can empower a shy person to speak out, you may well elicit a rather novel idea or approach to a problem you're trying to solve. My shyness has made me think more, observe more, learn more, and I believe it has made me more determined to succeed. As a child, I couldn't comfortably perform or be the loud kid, but I could channel all my energy into learning new skills. In the workplace, I've been able to focus on what I want and find clever ways to get it – without being the loudest or the most flamboyant. Society favours boldness and confidence, but quiet people can also get what they want by employing a more strategic approach.

Facebook CEO Mark Zuckerberg's shyness was dramatised in the film *The Social Network* based on him founding the company, but has been confirmed by his close colleague and friend, Sheryl Sandberg – COO of Facebook. 'He is shy and introverted and he often does not seem very warm to people who don't know him, but he is warm,' she said in a *New York Times* interview.[6] 'He really cares about the people who work here.' Perhaps if Zuckerberg hadn't been shy and introverted, he wouldn't have locked himself away to build Facebook, which is now the world's biggest social network, with 2.4 billion users.[7] Of course, there is a certain irony to the head of the most used social network being someone who shies away from socialising himself. But then, as we'll discuss in chapter 7, the online world is a shy person's friend.

● ●

Jan-ai El-Goni, vocalist and songwriter, on shyness:

I'm not sure if I was shy as a child. There were always lots of family and friends in my house as a child so I think I had to adapt quite quickly and engage, so didn't really have a chance to be shy. I knew and liked most of the people I interacted with. I think I was more quiet as a child. I liked to read and listen to conversations rather than join in.

I remember my favourite spot in my nan's house was behind her rocking chair. I'd sit there hidden between the sofa next to the rocking chair and listen and watch the goings-on in the living room without being seen. Like a little den.

In my late teens, I decided I wanted to be a performer. But I rarely performed in public. It got worse in uni. Crippling shyness was most present there. I love singing but doing it in front of people was a slow process. I would not go to lessons because I was so anxious and shy to sing in front of people.

In every performance there is an element of your innermost feelings being exposed. There is always a level of shyness involved with putting yourself out there to be judged. But in that shyness is a vulnerability that I think is necessary to connect with an audience. We've all felt like that before, even if we feel shy because we've done something good and it's being praised.

Ultimately, the feelings of connection and freedom of expression of singing outweigh the feelings of shyness, or in extreme cases: anxiety. I know that, so I push myself to get the job done. You can tell I'm internally stressed though because of the amount I sweat!

I use a combination of tools if I feel a bit overwhelmed. I'll go somewhere quiet and breathe for a minute, or give myself a pep talk in the toilet and down a shot. Each day is different.

I'm mostly shy now in social situations where I only know a few people. I'm really bad at small talk so I revert back to being a kid sometimes and just sit back and nod and smile because I don't know what to say.

I find shouty people quite difficult. I can't get my words out when I'm talking to really boisterous, super-animated people. My boyfriend says I am one though, so who knows?

I think for me shyness has two sides. I feel shy or awkward most of the time, but I also like talking to people and finding out their stories. I approach things a bit like 'I feel shy, but I can't stand here like a lemon: go and talk to one person.' That usually leads to a conversation that ends up involving more people, and before I know it I'm not feeling shy any more. Not gonna lie, though, there is usually an alcoholic beverage in my hand the whole time.

6

But confidence helps too

Believe in your flyness . . .
conquer your shyness.

Kanye West

When I was nineteen, I was in a bar one night and this guy called Dave came over and asked me to fill out a questionnaire about alcohol. I was tipsy and sitting down, so said yes. I got my friends to fill one out too. While I was ticking the multiple choice answers, I asked Dave how he'd got this job; it seemed pretty chilled. He said he was hired by a market research company. I said I'd like a job too and he gave me his business card. I was soon hired to go into bars and pubs and ask people to fill out questionnaires about booze and cigarettes (I know; morally questionable. But this was a while back when you were still allowed to smoke inside and there weren't photos of tar-filled lungs on fag packets; it was a different time).

But, after being sent the paper survey and the instructions, plus a bag of lighters to give out as an incentive, it occurred to me that I'd now have to walk into a bar and approach people, cold, who were mid-conversation, to ask them to do something they probably didn't want to do. This was, as jobs go, up there with one of the worst for a shy person. But they'd offered to pay me £150 a night, and that was a *lot* of money to me back then. So I decided to 'feel the fear and do it anyway'. I think my mum had actually recently given me the self-help book with that name, so perhaps it had taught me that the only way to overcome a fear is to face it head-on.

I went into the first bar and asked someone to fill out a survey in exchange for a heavy silver lighter. They said yes. I asked another person, and they said yes, too. Others said no, and told me to piss off with their eyes, but I realised that didn't matter. If someone didn't want to do it, that was fine. As long as I got enough 'yeses', I'd still be paid. I ploughed on through the evening, gaining confidence with every interaction. And this then became my job alongside studying at university. Soon, I'd helped Dave to recruit another twenty or so students, and we all got these surveys filled out for him, and the market research company who employed him. I ended up going abroad for the job, became a mystery 'drinker' (ordering alcohol and taking notes on how it was served, then drinking it – great job) and got free tickets to music festivals in exchange for carrying out some market research.

According to research, men and women who work in sales have the lowest levels of shyness.[1] This may be because people who choose to work in sales already feel more confident, so know they'll do well in this role – but it could also be because if you take a role in sales, you'll then have to behave in accordance with the expectations of what a salesperson should do: sell. So while the researchers didn't determine whether people choose workplaces to fit their levels of shyness, they believe that there will be some effect of the workplace on shyness; i.e. the job you do may impact your general shyness. And this is consistent with how I started to feel after taking that job with Dave. The more evenings I spent approaching people in bars and asking them to help with the market research, the less shy I became in general.

When I asked *Grazia*'s deputy editor Rosamund Dean, who regularly interviews celebrities, if she could remember any who were particularly shy, she said that almost all actors say they were shy as kids and that's why their parents put them into performing arts classes; to make them more confident.

Her husband, Jonathan Dean, also interviews actors and musicians for his job at the *Sunday Times*, and said:

> I have spoken to a lot of actors and actresses –
> and, indeed, musicians – and one thing that many
> of them bring up is how, at school, they were shy.

It is a cliché of the very famous, who perform for a living. Always the same pattern. They were in a shell at school and so their parents signed them up for drama classes in order to break that shell and, fast forward thirty years, they're winning an Oscar. It makes sense – forcing a child onto a stage is certainly a way to make them speak. It is interesting too – especially given the extrovert nature of what they do for a living. However, so frequent were these instances of actors and actresses talking about their shyness, that I haven't actually included those quotes in the finished piece for years. It is such a part of many stories that it wasn't really that interesting to the individuals any more.

But while it may be a little trite to include notes on shyness in every celebrity interview, it does occasionally make the final edit, which is how I came to learn that Nicole Kidman is shy. 'The one thing I struggle with is [getting] through my shyness,' she told *Backstage Magazine*, 'because if I'm willing to speak up and not be obedient all the time, then I'm free and I do much better work. But if I haven't worked for a long time, my shyness comes back and I'm a little rigid almost and scared. So it helps me to work a lot because it frees me.'[2] This notion of experiencing shyness but not letting it hold you back is crucial in terms of living with shyness. It's OK to acknowledge it and for it to be part of you, and it may even add an edge to Kidman with her acting, but when you feel it's preventing you from doing good work, it needs to be addressed.

Irish actor Andrew Scott, who rose to fame playing the role of Jim Moriarty in the BBC series *Sherlock*, started drama classes aged eight. 'I was very shy and had a bit of a lisp,' he said in an interview with the *Evening Standard*, 'so I went to drama classes. And for some reason, even though it was terrifying, having to stand up in front of other kids, I really loved it.'[3] He still feels shy now, sometimes, but says: 'I've learned that I can't be. You have to overcome it.' Like Kidman, he knows that shyness will hold him back with his acting. The same trait that led him to that career originally has the potential to end his career, if he lets it.

Comedy actor Jim Carrey has also experienced shyness. 'I know this sounds strange, but as a kid, I was really shy. Painfully shy. The turning point was freshman year, when I was the biggest geek alive. No one, I mean no one, even talked to me.' And Johnny Depp still feels it now: 'I'm shy, paranoid, whatever word you want to use. I hate fame. I've done everything I can to avoid it.' So there are these A-list actors, amassing a fortune from securing well-paid, respected acting jobs, and yet they're shy. But it's possible that their shyness is the reason they started acting in the first place; it goes back to facing your fears in order to move forward in life, as well as pushing yourself out of your comfort zone.

Once the shy kid has started acting classes, and realised they feel passionately about pursuing a career onstage or camera, they are not only using these new skills to propel them into a more confident state immediately and in the long-term, but they are also setting themselves up, if successful, to experience lower levels of shyness as adults. Because people with high-status occupations and high income brackets get to this stage by adapting their personality; we're not simply born to either be successful or not.[4] Hollywood fame aside, just being employed will help people in terms of shyness. The human interaction, daily purpose and financial independence all impact a person's confidence.

Emma Gannon – *Sunday Times* bestselling author and host of award-winning podcast *Ctrl Alt Delete* – has chosen a career that involves social interaction and putting herself in the spotlight. 'A part of my job – that I have actively chosen – is meeting new people/introducing myself/doing talks/workshops,' she says, 'and thankfully I am not shy socially at all otherwise my job would be much harder or at least less enjoyable, but I love meeting new people and don't have any issues "mingling" or whatever.' Though she does crave time alone and says she can 'definitely be quiet/introverted, for example when you're stuck at a very long wedding with people you hardly know and just cannot wait for it to be over etc. Or after doing a talk I can feel quite drained and would rather go straight home. If I'm around too many talkative people for too long I need to go home and re-charge/be alone and my boyfriend has learned that "alone time" in the house doesn't mean anything personal/ bad towards him!'

Again, the question arises about whether a quieter person chooses a career that will help them to build confidence or whether the confidence comes first and the career choice naturally follows. Either way, immersing yourself in social situations and trying out different jobs that require you to learn new skills and challenge you in different ways is sure to have an impact on your general shyness levels. The Shyness Study found that spending a lot of time in familiar, socially un-challenging contexts (e.g. being at home) may result in higher mean levels of shyness.[5] But in contrast, lower shyness may be linked to higher chances of obtaining a job in the first place. Either way, putting yourself forward for events and career options that throw you way out of your comfort zone is likely to help with your confidence, as writer Alex Holder discovered.

Holder grew up in Liverpool and attended a state school that didn't encourage performance of any kind. 'Showing off was something you didn't do,' she says. 'There was no debate team, no drama club.' She feels this contributed to her fear of standing up in front of people and presenting. 'To even talk out loud in class was "out there",' she remembers. But when she moved to London for university, she was surrounded by people who'd been educated differently: 'These people had been told they were allowed to speak up in a room; that their opinion was valuable.' She became, for the first time, aware of her education: 'There were things I didn't know. And my pronunciation of words was different, also how I structured sentences. Maybe it was called out for everyone, but I remember it stinging and not wanting to speak out again.'

On top of feeling different to the students around her in terms of class and education, there was a confidence divide. 'I remember people standing up to talk and thinking: how do you do this?' she says. Initially she thought they just had a natural ability to do public speaking, but she then discovered that it was in fact down to the training they'd received at school and learned that therefore, she could be trained too. She found techniques to help her prepare for presentations, like learning it off by heart. She'd also film herself on her computer as she practised – and would keep going over it until she could deliver it perfectly. She became so proficient that someone commented on her presenting skills, telling her how good she was, perhaps not realising she'd spent five days preparing, she says.

So she'd nailed class presentations, but she then faced a new challenge when she entered the workplace. Holder got a job in advertising, working her way up to creative director, and would have to present her ideas to a room of people and convince them that her thinking was good. There were also group reviews, which felt competitive. It was a tough environment to work in – all working on the same brief, with ideas being 'shot down' daily – and her confidence started to dip. Added to that was the fact that it was a very male environment and once again, this made her feel 'slightly "other"'. She remembers lots of tears, imposter syndrome, and not feeling she was funny enough. And regularly being in 'panic mode'.

When Holder fluffed a presentation due to nerves, and someone else stepped in to take over, she decided it was time to make a change. A friend had done a stand-up comedy course and told her that others were on the course not because they were planning a career in stand-up, but for confidence-building. It felt like the most scary thing Holder could do – stand up in front of a room of people and perform comedy – so she signed up for a six-week course. 'It was awful,' she says. 'But I knew what I was putting myself through and wanted to do it. I thought: if I do get to the end and do a gig in a pub – I know something will change.' Each week, she'd write and perform a mini gig in front of her classmates. 'There was a safe space created. We were all failing together and that's why it worked. I learned that comedians who look really casual – chatting away, confident – they've probably performed that gig 100 times. Most people could probably look confident with that amount of practice.'

But then came the time for her to do the end-of-course gig. 'I've never felt more sick,' she says, 'more nervous. I can remember the carpet of the pub, standing there, bracing myself. But I learned the piece off by heart and delivered it.' And it was fine. But more importantly, Holder then felt she'd combated her fear of public speaking. 'It's like that TV show *Faking It*,' she says. 'Once they took a really shy girl – a classically trained musician – and turned her into a DJ. They made her stand at the top of a hill and scream really loudly, and got strangers in the street to listen to her music. That was my idea of hell. And has always stuck with me. But her transformation was amazing.' Holder now does regular public speaking gigs as part of her job. And although the years in advertising were gruelling, she says: 'It was amazing training for life; I feel very resilient as a freelancer now because of it.'

Jess Jones – writer, comedian and influencer, known on Instagram as @thefatfunnyone – has also used comedy to combat her shyness, though her story is different to Holder's, in that she felt confident as a child. 'I loved the stage and performing. Some would have described me as "precocious" but not really shy.' She would get nervous before performing in school plays or shows, and didn't feel as confident when meeting a large group of new people, but it didn't hold her back. However, she was bullied as an adult, in the workplace. 'This certainly had an impact on my confidence,' she says. 'It made me more cautious and wary of what others were thinking, and knocked my confidence significantly so I became shy, withdrawn and less myself.' But she was determined to overcome it, so channelled her 'inner child' – the confidence she had, 'and the conviction that I was wonderful at what I did', and recently performed her first sell-out comedy gig. She's now planning a UK-wide tour.

'I get nervous, some situations still make me incredibly anxious,' she says, 'but I am so fortunate I've always had such wonderful audiences and I think due to the nature of my shows – motivational comedy – people are there to be inspired as well as laugh so I don't tend to receive any negativity. I always prepare myself by remembering that not everyone is going to like it, negative reviews may happen . . . but they don't define me.'

It seems that whether we are shy as children or develop shyness due to bullying or trauma later in life, shyness can be both malleable and multifaceted. We can use the traits that often accompany our shyness to our advantage (the observational skills, empathy, quiet determination). And we can push through the elements of our shyness that hold us back – by getting on the stage, or putting ourselves forward for the job. But it is also layered. By which I mean that there is the shyness we feel inside; the shyness we reveal to others through our behaviour – and then the shyness that other people diagnose as they observe us.

For example, I was interested to read an Instagram post by Alix Walker, *Stylist*'s editor-at-large, about when the magazine was launched ten years previously and on the team was Natasha Tomalin-Hall who Walker remembers '. . . starting out as a shy intern and becoming the sweariest, angriest colleague.' Tomalin-Hall wound up as *Stylist*'s art director before leaving to set up her own branding consultancy. She's now creative director at *You* magazine. I wanted to know whether she actually *felt* shy as an intern at *Stylist*, or if that was just how she was perceived.

'I actually didn't think I was that shy,' she says, 'but I certainly wasn't my full self for about a year, although my colleagues clearly thought I was a bit of a shy oddball. I actually think that looking back I was trying to gauge how to be in a new work environment. Fully taking stock of the people around me before I let them get to know my true personality (loud, sweary, angry and pretty theatrical all round).' She remembers feeling shy as a child – '. . . with children of my own age. But not really that shy with adults. This may have been due to the fact that my parents were older parents and I was an only child' – but it didn't hold her back because her mum wouldn't let it. 'I used to hate doing any kind of summer schools or group activities where I had to meet a new group of kids,' she says. 'Mum always forced me into it with the promise that I would end up really enjoying it . . . she was always right.'

Tomalin-Hall also remembers being 'very shy' in classroom situations. 'My reports constantly said that I was always too shy to put my hand up in class for fear of getting something wrong.' But she became more confident as she went through her teens and into her 20s. 'I actually think that attention from boys in my teens helped me conquer my shyness,' she says, and notes that her shyness depended on the situation. For instance, there was the time she went on a skiing trip with an ex-boyfriend. 'He loved skiing, I hated it,' she says. 'But I went to ski school to try and learn and take part. I was painfully shy and unconfident on the slopes, timid and a bit weird. On the last day all the pupils from the ski school went to the pub after to celebrate what we'd learned and obviously my true "theatrical" self came out. They couldn't believe the person on the slopes and the person in front of them now in a social environment were one and the same.'

As she got older, and became more successful with her career, Tomalin-Hall felt the shyness dropping away. 'I would say I'm hardly ever shy in situations any more,' she says. 'I do quite a lot of public speaking – although that has never really bothered me as I did a lot of acting at school – and I have to be confident and authoritative in my role at work otherwise people doubt you. The only time I ever feel a little shy is when I'm art directing on shoots. I'm sure this is down to not doing it enough earlier on in my career. I now do it on a weekly basis, and as a result have become much more confident with it. Having confidence is the key to overcoming shyness.'

So we fake it until we feel it, and then we really do start to find certain situations more bearable. I've found that in terms of public speaking – this is almost certainly every shy person's worst nightmare, in terms of career – the more I do it, the less scared I become. Like Alex Holder, I massively over-prepare. I practise, take notes onstage with me and make sure that I'm ready for any eventuality in terms of the questions that might be thrown my way. But while I still get a little jittery before going onstage, it's nothing compared to the first public speaking gig I had at Stylist Live, in front of 300 women. I spent months preparing, came out in a rash and felt like it was the scariest thing I'd ever done in my life. This is not an exaggeration. I was there to talk about 'the morning routines of successful people' with celebrity chef Jasmine Hemsley, and Cassandra Stavrou, founder of Propercorn. I had massive imposter syndrome and was utterly dreading it. But the preparation – physical and mental; imagining myself on the stage performing brilliantly, not turning red and losing track of my thought process – meant it went fine. I even enjoyed it.

Just prior to the publication of my first book, *The Freelance Mum*, we had a launch for women who'd contributed to the book. I'd prepared a small speech and felt a bit nervous about delivering it but wanted to say my piece. Everyone gathered, I half read from the notes but had also practised it and memorised parts, and again, I quite enjoyed it. What I noted, when looking at photos from the event, was that I'd subconsciously adopted the classic 'superwoman pose' – standing with legs apart, hands on waist. So in the photos I look really confident, even if I didn't feel it. When you look confident, people believe you are. And when others think you are, and tell you so, it's possible to adopt this persona they've created of you. It's a wonderful self-fulfilling prophecy.

Often, facing your fear is the only way to shrink it.

Here are some tips for dealing with the areas of work-life that shy people may well dread.

i. Public speaking and work presentations

Remember the five Ps: plan, prepare, practise, physical presence, present.

Plan: do your research. Fact check. Write down what you're going to say. Get it all down and then think about separating it into bullet points or subheadings, so that you can use these to refer to throughout.

Prepare: Think about your presentation or performance. Where's it being held? Do you need to wrap up warm or wear light cotton clothes because it's taking place in a stuffy meeting room? Imagine yourself delivering your piece: how do you want to look and feel? Make this happen; looking the part will help you to feel the part. And wearing the right gear will also ensure you don't get hot and sweaty or feel cold and shaky. Avoid itchy clothes and jewellery that will get in your way. These may sound like minor adjustments, but on the day, they will matter.

Practise: Once you've got it down, say it out loud. Change or remove any parts that don't work so well when spoken. Say it again and if it sounds better, keep that version. Now say it again. And again. Film yourself saying it out loud. Repeat, repeat, repeat until you know it very well.

Physical presence: This is about body language and movement. Will you be sitting or standing? If you're sitting, try to keep your body open to the room (e.g. not folding your arms on your chest). Make eye contact with the people you're addressing. This will help you to see that they're listening; they're interested in what you're saying. If you're standing, it's OK to move around, or to stand still. Equally, some gesticulation can work, but don't overdo it. Try to talk as if you're telling a story to your friends, and this will make it look and feel more natural.

Present: On the day, keep in mind that almost everyone feels a little nervous when all eyes are on them; it's natural. It's also OK to make a mistake and correct it, or to refer to your notes if you've lost your line of thought. You're human; so is your audience.

ii. Dealing with rejection

I have been rejected *so many times*. Ignored, received a blunt 'no' and been told I'm not good enough. At first, in my early 20s and fresh out of university, I'd be amazed if someone didn't respond. Now I'm older and wiser and know that they don't respond because they're too busy, the timing isn't right, or my work/idea isn't right for them. This doesn't mean it's not good. So it's important to continue pushing it out. After trying lots of times, and not succeeding, it might be worth tweaking or moving on. Just don't take it personally; every perceived failure takes you closer to success, as you're constantly learning about how to be better at what you do.

And if you're feeling as if you're never going to succeed, just remember that J. K. Rowling sent the *Harry Potter* manuscript out to every mainstream publisher and it was rejected by all but the last one. So persevere.

Here are some ideas on dealing with rejection from Twitter:

Publisher Liz Gough – @lizzgough – says: Don't be embarrassed or ashamed to feel down for a few days. Then, head high, keep going, re-examine your strategy/ focus. Re-motivate yourself by talking to partner/friends. Optimism!

Freelance journalist Bianca Barratt – @bianca_barratt – says: In my experience, rejection and failure always leads to something better – whether that's growth or a more suitable opportunity. To deal with it in the moment I give my ego a moment of self-pity (!) then change my mindset to see it as a course correction rather than failure.

National campaign manager Jack Jolly – @jackwjolly – says: Seek feedback where you can. The majority of rejection is out of your hands (budgets, wrong timing, wrong people involved). If it's work, you are not your work – try and separate the i from the idea.

Photographer Penny Wincer – @pennywincer – says: Name the emotions you're feeling. It can help with not over-identifying or ruminating on them. 'I'm feeling crap about not getting that job' is much gentler than 'I must be crap because I didn't get that job'. It really helps.

Writer and academic Dr Pragya Agarwal – @DrPragya Agarwal – says: It is tough to not take it personally. And it is OK to acknowledge the feeling of dejection and grief over not getting something that we really wanted. But then, a growth mindset for me is seeing why that rejection happened, what I can learn from it and then moving on.

iii. Pitching

Coach and entrepreneur Suzy Aswhorth shares some tips on pitching – for a promotion, new job, commission.

1. Start to build up your confidence muscle by writing down everything you do now and noting how the skills you have will support you in your new move.

2. Think proactively, imagine that you already have the job and think about three key things you would want to bring your attention to during your first 90 days, and why these things will make a positive difference to the team/company. This will not only help you feel excited about the impact you have the potential to make, but will give you some great golden nuggets you can share in your interview.

3. Rather than think about your shyness as a weakness, think about how your personality traits have served you in the past. Playing to your strengths – rather than trying to be someone you are not – is always powerful. So, if you know that people always feel relaxed around you, because you don't have a desire to try to steal the limelight, say that.

iv. Networking

Alice Olins, founder of Step Up Club – a career coaching and membership group for women in business – shares three tips for networking, as a shy person:

1. **Change your perspective:** Networking is a game of selling yourself to others, so reframe that thought. Rather, think of it as a space and chance to help others: you have knowledge and connections that

they likely don't and this is your way of sharing what and who you know. Remember, networking isn't about becoming more popular, it's a strategic game of give and take. Give first, and the 'taking' (or asking) will always feel easier.

2. **Talk to a large group:** It might sound counter-intuitive, but introverts, or those who feel shy, often find it easier to speak to a group, rather than getting caught in lots of one-to-ones. If you want to meet more people in your company or wider industry, organise a Zoom event that opens a discussion in an area within which you feel extremely comfortable. This way, you can introduce the topic, bring others together, invite and answer questions and show yourself as an expert without having to have any awkward conversations.

3. **Be online:** This may sound like the most obvious piece of advice, but get online. Networking doesn't have to involve formal emails, or stilted telephone conversations. You can bypass these and remain present and connected by using LinkedIn Messenger, Instagram, whatever social media fits your work. Sending a DM feels a lot less daunting than meeting someone in person, plus you can introduce some personality too, which will make you memorable.

Other good ideas: share links to articles that others might enjoy, or tag people in social media groups you're both in; we live in a golden time for connections without having to leave the comfort of your sofa. Abuse this as much as you can.

v. Forming new relationships

Holly June Smith, life coach, celebrant and speaker, says:

One simple way to form new relationships in the workplace is to ask people if they have ten minutes to tell you more about their work. You might meet someone in the staff canteen and say: 'I've just joined X team, what do you do here, I'd love to learn about it?'. Or if that feels too bold, you could email someone and say: 'I'm interested in learning more about your department/area of the business, do you have ten mins to tell me more about it?'

When it comes to meeting, this could be popping out for coffee, or it could be just chatting at their desk. Ask lots of questions about them and their role, and how it works with yours. Take a notebook with you, and it can be nice to end by asking: 'Who else do you think I should meet?'

In 2012 I took a junior website assistant role at a charity with hundreds of employees. I'd never worked anywhere this big before and the organisation had lots of divisions that I didn't understand at all. By using this approach I benefited in two ways. One, I got to meet lots of people and grow my network in the company, it felt great to be able to say hello to lots of people as I moved around the building. Two, I learned lots about the organisation that helped me, my team and our projects. I was able to connect people, add lots of value and ultimately be promoted.

vi. Asserting yourself

Julia Davies is a person-centred trained bereavement counsellor. And my mother. I've always admired her ability to deflect any questions or situations that she isn't ready to answer or deal with, so I asked her to share three tips for asserting yourself. These can be used in the workplace, but also in everyday life.

During my counselling training I picked up three good tips which have helped me to assert myself:

1. I learned to be an active listener without interrupting. This makes me appear more calm.

2. I use open body language. When I feel anxious my natural inclination is to protect myself, by crossing

my arms, crossing my legs. By sitting there with legs and arms uncrossed I appear more relaxed and start to feel easier too.

3. Rather than directly label the other person as a bully or a tormentor, I talk about their behaviour: 'When you tell me I am weak I feel badly let down.' This reply then makes it more difficult for that person to retaliate.

vii. People-pleasing tendencies

Tamu Thomas, a former social worker who now coaches women and runs the wellness brand Three Sixty, says that shyness can sometimes lead to a shrinking of our lives. 'The challenge is that being "shy" becomes a pattern that gets confused with fear,' she says. 'So clients become fearful of life and apply confining labels to themselves. They get so attached to the behaviour becoming a pathology they don't have space to learn how to care for themselves from a loving place. Social interactions are written off or they start replaying interactions and looking for things they did wrong.'

This can be tricky in the workplace, as shy people might then be more easily manipulated, in a bid to fit in. 'It can bring out people-pleasing tendencies,' Thomas says. 'This is going to sound bold, but I have found that beneath the people-pleasing is manipulation. Rather than stating needs, people-pleasing becomes a way to get people to like them or see them as useful or worth having around. I think this is because as a society we have been led to believe that humans need to be extroverted and gregarious to be worthy.'

In those situations – perhaps when your boss or a colleague has sensed a shyness, and is taking advantage in some way; picking up on the 'people-pleasing' tendencies and giving you the work no one else wants to do, for instance – it's important to return to those assertiveness techniques outlined above. When you're asked to complete a task that doesn't fit within your work remit – you can always say: 'I'm going to have a think about this and get back to you by the end of the hour/day/week.' Take your time, and devise a response. You can always put it in writing, if that feels more comfortable than confronting someone in person.

As a shy person, creating a career in a world that celebrates extroverts and confidence, it can feel as if there isn't space for us, or we'll never get quite as far. But that's simply not true. It's about focusing on your attributes, skills and experience and where you are succeeding – not failing – and continuing to push forward, quietly. This includes being honest about your needs, learning how to confront people and situations that you find difficult – in a way that works for you – and ensuring that no one takes advantage of you. You are worthy of success.

7

The online world is a shy person's friend

The way you overcome shyness is to become so wrapped up in something that you forget to be afraid.

Lady Bird Johnson

When I was in my late teens, I spent a summer looking after two boys on my street. One day, the mother came in and said: 'You're young, you'll know the answer to this: what's a blog?' I didn't know what it was, so I asked my boyfriend at the time, and he explained. A few years later, on finishing university and having been rejected by every local newspaper I'd applied to for a journalism job, I decided to launch my own blog. I loved that I could write whatever I wanted and then hit 'publish'. I didn't have to check with a teacher or tutor or editor. I didn't need a job at a magazine or newspaper to get my writing out in the public domain. What I hadn't realised was that not only would this be the start of a new career for me, but that it had opened the doors to a whole new way of presenting myself to the world: through the internet.

And so when I went on to launch a digital parenting magazine, I published articles online and shared them on social media. Soon, that website was getting thousands of hits each month, but I wasn't having to do any real-life presenting; it was all online. This fitted perfectly with my inner performer and outer shyness. I felt like when I was doing any kind of 'presenting' online – on Instagram Stories or during Facebook Live sessions – I was no longer inhibited. I could be the person I felt I was, and am, but without the fear I might have felt if I were doing a live performance in front of a real audience. Also, with it being online, I was able to practise more. So while at first it definitely felt awkward and embarrassing recording myself as I talked into my iPhone, in time I became more confident to perform in this way, and now I feel almost totally at ease.

Victoria Hargreaves (@victoriaemes on Instagram) has well over 100,000 followers, and over 20,000 of them watch the Stories she puts out most days. So she has a lot of eyes on her, online. And her comedy videos, where she dresses up in leotards and galavants around her house, have gone viral and been picked up by national newspaper websites. She swears, talks about her private parts and generally seems completely uninhibited. So when she told me that actually, she's really shy, hates filming in front of anyone, even her husband, and only does it when she's home alone, I was shocked. I had no idea. And then I realised that I'm the same: I feel self-conscious walking down the street filming myself so I, too, only tend to do it when

I'm home alone. But I also don't like having my family as an audience.

'Strangely enough, I am actually really incredibly shy in real life,' Victoria said. 'So the way I speak on my Stories – you would only ever really see that side of me if you knew me well. If I was to meet you in any other situations, I either probably wouldn't speak, because I'd just be too shy to speak, or you'd think I was fucking rude. That's the feedback I've had. But it's funny, because I've always been shy; I've been shy since I was a child, but Instagram has given me this whole new confidence in myself, and belief in myself, that I didn't really know existed. But the only reason that's happened is because I've put myself out there, and laid everything bare – on a plate – and I have had some shit from it along the way, but the overwhelming majority of responses I've had have been positive.'

What Victoria describes here reinforces the notion that being shy doesn't mean you can't be brave, courageous or creative. It just means that you might have a different comfort zone, or favour particular ways of expressing yourself. Online, for instance. And Tamu Thomas corroborates this. She says it bugs her that people often conflate shyness with insecurity. 'I don't think that introverts or shy people are naturally insecure,' she says. 'They just have a style they prefer that energises them.' And this feels right to me.

That you may feel less comfortable in certain environments, as a shy person, but it doesn't mean you are generally insecure. For instance, you might be quietly confident but not feel inclined to speak out. Or perhaps you shy away from presenting in work meetings in the office, but find that when they're taking place on Zoom, you're more willing to perform.

i. Social interaction online

The advent of social networking websites like Facebook marked a change in how we communicate with one another. While some face-to-face contact is still hugely important for our mental health and general well-being, platforms like Facebook gave shy people an opportunity to engage in a way that might have felt a lot more natural to them. And no wonder, considering Facebook's founder, Mark Zuckerberg, is famously shy. So he created a digital platform that meant instead of having to physically approach a new group of colleagues or mums at the school gate, for instance, you could instead login online, join community groups and start the communication this way.

And there's an argument for beginning relationships online, as it might be safer and more productive – for adults, at least – than meeting for the first time in person. This is why dating websites like Match.com and apps like

Tinder took off: they give people the opportunity to screen each other before actually meeting up. Similarly, apps like Peanut and Mush, that connect like-minded women, and mums, looking for friendship. Because if the conversation starts online and you can discover shared interests, this removes the pressure of having to perform on the spot, in order to make a good first impression. After all, studies have shown that we have just seven seconds to impress a stranger on first meeting, which puts shy people at a disadvantage.

But in terms of whether digital communication, in general, is healthy for shy people – the research is conflicting.

A 2007 study on shyness, internet use and personality found that – not surprisingly – the more shy participants were, the more they favoured online communication.[1] The conclusion was that while the internet offered shy people a medium through which to communicate with the world around them, their internet use might be problematic because it was being used to make up for a deficit in their real-life social life. By establishing virtual friendships, they might be hoping that this would relieve feelings of loneliness and depression. Also, the shyer a person was, the longer they tended to stay online and think about the internet.

But a study produced three years later, on 'Shyness and Online Social Networking Services', investigated the association between the use of websites like Facebook and friendship quality for individuals varying in shyness,[2] and reported contrary results. They found that individuals high in shyness reported stronger associations between Facebook use and friendship quality. Facebook use, however, was unrelated to loneliness among highly shy individuals. Therefore, they concluded: 'online social networking services may provide a comfortable environment within which shy individuals can interact with others.'

Kemi Omijeh, a child and adolescent psychotherapist and mental health consultant, agrees that the online world can be beneficial for shy people. 'I think technology can be great and preferential for a shy person,' she says. 'By and large I think communicating online keeps social interaction going, it expands your world, and we all could do with that. It's not communicating online versus communicating in person, both have a role to play in socialising and both can complement each other well. Lockdown showed us that it is very possible to keep our relationships and interactions going online, however we missed real-life contact for a reason.'

ii. Working online

Until 2020, the workplace was designed for outgoing employees. The traditional boardroom is set up so that speaking out in meetings requires the loudest voice, and for that person to accept that all heads will turn. What that meant for me, when I worked in a corporate office environment, is that I just didn't speak up. I read Sheryl Sandberg's *Lean In* and tried to take a seat at the table, but that table wasn't designed for me and my personality. I'd find myself desperately trying to think of something to contribute in meetings, but any intelligent thoughts I might have had, if I'd been on my own at a desk, were blocked by fear. So I stayed quiet. Sometimes, I'd collate my thoughts in an email, post-meeting, but often the moment had passed. It was too late.

This may have contributed to my keenness to work freelance from home, and then set up my own business. Because this meant I was in charge of meetings. And now, they mostly take place over email. Like many shy people, I like to have time to think about my response rather than being put on the spot. So email and messenger services work well for me. This meant that when the pandemic hit, my work life wasn't hugely impacted. Having three kids at home with us full-time made things challenging, but in terms of the way I work: I continued with my emails, social media groups and running online courses.

But I was interested in how others adapted during this time, and it occurred to me that some shy workers may have blossomed during the Zoom meetings of lockdown. Claire Vivyan Roberts is a corporate career coach and she believes the online version of life has been a great equaliser. 'We are all in the same box now,' she says. With a Zoom conference, each participant has their equally-sized screen but also, they are sitting in the comfort of their own homes. Roberts believes this might have made it a bit easier 'to overcome shyness and intimidation, and to have a voice, especially in a professional context.'

Psychologist Dr Sam Akbar, however, wonders if the intensity of Zoom 'could actually be more unappealing to some shy people, as it really puts you on the spot'. She says that 'Perhaps the online space does help people come out of their shell in terms of expressing themselves online, but perhaps not always through video?' But she makes an interesting point on the social element of office life that may be a challenge for shy people. 'I wonder if what is actually helpful about the online space is that you don't have to do so much social chitchat before and after a meeting,' she says, 'and maybe that helps you not use up precious energy.'

Ingrid Fernandez is a lawyer, the founder of Dec + Dash legal consultancy, and she is regularly invited to speak on panels. She says: 'As a shy person, I've historically found connecting online easier than in person. However, during the pandemic, when event gigs have all been online, I've found it much harder to connect with people than I did at in-person events. Perhaps it's because when I did speaking events in person, I could put on my "speaker" hat, and interact and connect with people with the confidence of being a speaker. Whereas when I'm a speaker at online events, I don't have that same veneer of protection and find connecting in group settings near impossible.'

Meanwhile, divorce coach Lucy Williamson feels less shy online. 'This is partly because I often show up professionally online and I'm less shy in that capacity,' she says. 'It helps that clients are now familiar with Zoom etc., because that was nerve-wracking for some people before, on account of being new, different and fumbly. In a personal domain, I am still quite shy – unlikely to initiate a Zoom call with a group, and tempted to turn the camera off – but that's also due to Zoom fatigue and introversion. If I could meet people in real life, I'd jump at the chance.'

So, two professional women, both suddenly forced to work entirely online, who had fairly opposing experiences. This fits with confidence coach Vanessa Jones's analysis of the people she trained online during the pandemic. 'It's pretty much a 50/50 split in terms of whether it helps shy people,' she says. 'Some of my students have blossomed online – I think because they're in their own surroundings, their own safe space; whereas others feel intimidated by the camera, like the energy is extra focused on them somehow and it makes it more difficult. Also, it's definitely harder to read people's expressions and interest levels on a screen than in the room, and this can be off-putting for some people.'

For this reason, she prefers it when people leave their cameras on: 'Although obviously it's important to understand that not everyone finds it easy to do that,' she says, 'and each person's individual choice needs to be respected.'

In terms of whether the shift to working online during the pandemic will have had a largely positive or negative effect on shy people, we'll have to wait for the studies to be conducted. But anecdotally, it feels quite evenly split. Some shy people revelled in it; others found it harder. In much the same way that levels of shyness vary, and the circumstances in which shyness is useful – and then more challenging – also differ, this won't have been a blanket 'good' or 'bad' transition.

iii. Accessing services online

Dr Gina Liverton is a clinical psychologist in the NHS, and during the first lockdown, when she was only able to offer online or telephone sessions, she found people saying this would make them more likely to attend. 'Some people carried on wanting to meet virtually even when I could offer them face-to-face, once restrictions were lifted,' she says. 'For some, it was the flexibility, but for others there was an element of feeling daunted and experiencing social anxiety about the situation itself.'

'My perspective is that people who are shy or socially intro-verted are more likely to be put off by the more exposing aspects of therapy like meeting a new person and being incredibly candid with them,' she says, 'as well as poten-tially being around other people in the waiting room etc. For those people, starting a possibly daunting journey of therapy in the safety and comfort of their own home, where they feel confident and secure, I expect will be very tempting.'

She acknowledges that therapy is 'a pretty scary and weird prospect for many', and therefore suspects virtual therapy will continue to develop as an alternative option, for those who are more comfortable connecting in this way. 'It will be very helpful for those who are more timid or trepidatious about the whole process,' she says.

Interestingly, when I interviewed hypnotherapist Sophie Parker for a *Forbes* article on pivoting holistic services online during the pandemic, she said that while at first she wasn't sure it would be possible to deliver hypnotherapy sessions through a screen, she noticed that as the world grew more accustomed to being online in general, she found the enquiries flowing in. And she found that clients were committing more easily to making bookings. Partly because they wouldn't have the hassle of traveling to get there – but also because they could attend sessions more discreetly.

'You can't ignore the stigma that still persists with seeing a therapist,' she says. 'But now my clients don't have to worry about making excuses for why they need to leave the office on time, or what they're doing in their lunch break or after work, because they can flex appointments around their day. In short, you get the same experience online as in person but with the added benefit of seeing someone from the privacy and comfort of your own home.' So it might be that accessing services and therapies online may not only suit shy people but also those who want to use services without having to explain what they're doing to others.

In general, it feels to me that the online world creates a more balanced playing field for shy people. Because, while some of the shy people I've interviewed for this book have said forcing themselves out of their comfort zone was the only way to combat their shyness – in terms of public speaking, for instance – the psychologists have all suggested that the environments we're in should be adapted to nurture shy people, rather than shy people having to conform, or change themselves. So with Covid having possibly changed the office culture – and how we deliver various services – forever, we may be entering an era of shy people putting themselves forward for more opportunities, as they feel safer and more secure doing this over a screen than they do in person.

As a shy person, the internet can offer an opportunity to present yourself to the world however you'd like. If you're better with the written word than the spoken one, like me, this is your place. If you like performing but not live – vlogging, Instagram Stories and Facebook Lives will enable you to get your message out there without having to appear in front of an actual audience. And if you're happy to present over Zoom but come out in a cold sweat when it's even suggested you might present in an actual office, in front of several actual people, this is your time, too. But you also might find that once you start putting yourself forward for more opportunities online, and get in some practice

– you then feel more confident about then doing the #irl stuff: talks, presenting, networking. That's what happened to me.

• •

Robyn Wilder, journalist and author of *Reasons to be Fearful* (Ebury Press, 2022) on her shyness:

I had always described myself as shy. However, over the last twenty years I've been diagnosed with depression, various anxiety disorders, including social anxiety and ADHD. Since then I've never been sure what part of what I've always thought of as 'shyness' is actually down to social anxiety and/or sensory overload in social situations.

Mainly I never feel 'ready' for social interaction – whether I'm surprised in the street by a canvasser, or I'm attending a wedding I've known about for months.

I hate being the centre of attention so much that my husband and I (he's also shy) chose our wedding vows *based on how quickly we could say them*. I don't actually remember my vows – just that they had the fewest syllables possible, so I could minimise my time in the spotlight. God knows what sort of marriage I've actually signed up to.

Apparently I disliked being held by strangers even as a baby, and I remember hiding behind my mother's legs a lot when being introduced to anyone new. People dressed up as kids' characters were a particular terror (Disneyland was wasted on me).

When I was comfortable, though – at home, or with close friends – I could be noisy and rambunctious, and engage in raucous play. Which is, er, still the case.

In my teens I was a total girls' school cliché, and arrived at sixth form college with a new nose piercing, freshly dyed, waist-length, pillarbox-red hair – to try and dispel my last five years being intensely bullied. And I had an amazing time. I went to parties, joined a punk band, enthusiastically worked my way through a series of boyfriends and subsequently received disappointing A level results.

At the end of my teens I had a nervous breakdown, developed agoraphobia and became housebound for a period of four years. I would have panic attacks in public – and fear of embarrassing myself 'in front of people' played into that a great deal.

During these four years I realised that, as unpleasant as it was to live with a panic disorder, somehow not feeling constantly under pressure to perform socially in some way was incredibly freeing, and this realisation helped to inform my recovery from agoraphobia.

Shyness has held me back in my career – when I worked in office jobs, my managers would always send me on confidence courses, and the daily round of meetings would leave me drained (often at the expense of my actual job).

When I became a mum, I really had to push through my shyness – under orders from my doctor, to prevent my postnatal depression from getting any worse – and attend every baby group I could find locally. I was new to the area, so found myself introducing myself and my baby to rooms full of strangers (and their babies) several times a day. It was excruciating. I had no idea what to say. But repeated exposure did help ease my depression.

Forcing myself to socialise helped me develop a smoother, more confident, bubbly persona I can lay over my own identity for uncomfortable social situations. And this persona serves me now, in my work.

I'm a freelance writer and these days I work from home, often in pyjamas and with my children running around, and I far prefer this to office life. Sometimes I'm asked to speak in public, and it helps me to slip my social persona on, like a comfortable sweater.

Occasionally I'm also obliged to go 'for a coffee and a chat about a new project' (essentially a job interview where all aspects of the job and its criteria are unknown, and the interview is dressed up as a social event), which always fills me with horror – but where, again, my social persona comes in handy.

So shyness has negatives and positives. My social persona helps me move undetected through a world geared to non-shy people – but it also takes me days to recover from afterwards. I just wish more aspects of life were geared towards shy people – but that level of social change requires effective pressure at a grassroots level, and I can't see a 'Shy March' happening anytime soon.

8

You can overcome acute social anxiety

It appears that the mental powers of
infants are not as yet sufficiently developed
to allow of their blushing. Hence, also,
it is that idiots rarely blush.

Charles Darwin

What I didn't realise as a teenager was that I wasn't the only one who felt socially awkward. And the reason was that like me, my peers were doing such a good job of hiding it. It wasn't cool to feel 'shy' or to not want to be the funny one. So we either forced ourselves to be louder than we naturally wanted to be, or hid. I remember one friend telling me that she was getting ready for a fancy dress party and felt really nervous about dressing up and arriving on her own. So to overcome her nerves, she imagined she was me and waltzed into the party like someone confident. The irony of course being that I too would have felt self-aware and unconfident about all the attention I'd garner in that same situation, and yet I was doing such a good job of hiding it, she'd been totally misled.

One reason the people around me may have thought I was more confident than I felt was that by my teens, I was drinking enough alcohol to almost transform me socially.

I would drink for confidence. And at first, it was great. But the anxiety caused by a hangover can be horrific. I started having panic attacks during my A levels – largely, I believe, because of my lifestyle choices: booze, late nights. Being asked to read in front of my English class, or do a presentation, would fill me with dread. I'd find any way I could to avoid having to do it. The combination of teen-age hormones, the pressure of school exams, wanting to be socially accepted and my underlying shyness made those years quite riddled with anxiety.

I have vivid memories of walking down the street, or sitting on the Tube, hoping no one would look at me because I thought I'd blush. I was incredibly self-conscious. When I later started university, if I had a presentation, I'd sometimes take the day off to avoid it. But after graduating, and as I started looking for a proper job, I developed panic attacks. Again, not helped by my lifestyle and some relationship issues I was having. At this stage, I decided I needed to do something about my social anxiety so I started seeing a therapist who was trained in cognitive behavioural therapy (CBT). With her help, I was able to manage my – now daily – panic attacks. I started to understand that I had control over my thought process, and that this in turn affected how I felt in certain situations. Back then, it felt like survival; getting through each day. But I didn't realise I'd have these tools for life.

What I have found most interesting about researching this book is that so much of my experience is incredibly common and yet, until recent years, I felt so alone with my shyness – and later onset social anxiety. I opened Crozier and Alden's *Coping with Shyness and Social Phobia* and discovered an entire chapter on blushing.[1] I hadn't ever realised that this was something that other people felt so acutely aware of. When I was younger, I'd opt out of sharing my views for fear that the sudden turn of heads – in a classroom or social setting – would make me blush. It silenced me. And they explain their reason for devoting a chapter to blushing and the fear of blushing – medically known as erythophobia – is that for many people, this is their main concern. They may not feel shy or socially anxious, but they blush and this can be both visible and uncontrollable; it happens erratically and sometimes unexpectedly. And once you are blushing, the more you focus on it – the more it potentially intensifies.

In Charles Darwin's 1872 book *The Expression of the Emotions in Man and Animals*, he included a chapter on 'Self-attention – Shame – Shyness – Modesty: Blushing', as he found this 'the most peculiar and the most human of all expressions.'[2] He noted that monkeys redden from passion, but that there was no evidence otherwise of animals blushing. Furthermore, he said, while we can cause humans to laugh, weep or frown we cannot cause a blush,

'It is the mind which must be affected. Blushing is not only involuntary; but the wish to restrain it, by leading to self-attention, actually increases the tendency.' He wonders also why it is that babies redden from passion but don't blush; likewise 'idiots'. So there is nothing new about blushing.

Though blushing isn't just about a pinkening of the cheeks. It can also be experienced as a physical reaction, separate to the colour change. For instance, people with dark skin may not visibly blush, but they will feel it in their body. My friend Tamu Thomas is black and when we spoke about blushing, she said that she had used the term 'to blush' but had never considered its meaning. She assumed it just meant to feel shy/embarrassed. 'I didn't realise it was associated with going red in the face,' she said. And said that while a person with darker skin may not visibly redden in the same way, the bodily sensations will be the same. 'People of colour with darker skin may experience this as their cheeks getting warm or sweaty palms,' she said. 'But certainly, people of colour with dark skin – like my daughter – and friends and family with light brown skin do blush.'

The scientific explanation – 'the flow of blood through subcutaneous capillaries in the face and other areas where reddening occurs' – explains the physical reaction, but not how it links to the mind.[3] But looking at the situations in which people are more likely to blush, there are two that can be pinpointed. Firstly, it's when someone is anticipating that they are about to receive unwanted attention; so the blush precedes the event – and can even make that which the blusher is fearing, for instance suddenly having all eyes on them – actually more likely to receive this unwanted attention, as the blush may make people look and stare. Or secondly, when personal details are shared about us and we don't want them made public, or people are about to learn something about us that we don't want them to know. A child may blush when caught being naughty. Or an adult, when asked a question to which they don't know the answer.[4]

The best treatment for blushing is the same therapy that is recommended for shyness and social anxiety in general, which is CBT. It's the treatment I had when I was experiencing horrific panic attacks. I remember going to see the therapist and each week, I'd leave and say to myself, why am I still going? All I do is talk through my own issues and find my own solutions; she doesn't do anything. But I didn't realise that's what therapy actually is: the therapist acts as a facilitator, giving you the space to find solutions to your own issues. Though with CBT, it's a little more directive, as you are asked important questions to get you re-thinking your fear – e.g. blushing.

Judith Argent is a CBT therapist based in north London. I asked her why CBT is often so successful in treating patients with social anxiety, and how it works. 'It's about looking at how people see themselves as a social object and become very self-conscious,' she says, 'so you're working with that. I get people to recognise they carry out safety behaviours to feel better, as they feel it's unacceptable to be socially anxious.' By safety behaviours, Argent is referring to things like planning what you're going to say before attending an event, monitoring yourself, doing a post-mortem after a social engagement, looking to see if you're boring somebody.

She explains that people might have beliefs about how they think they should be in public – e.g. funny, say intelligent things, be focused all the time. And it's this belief system that she challenges. 'A big thing is reducing self-consciousness,' she says. 'They want to work out how they're coming across so they are then on the outside looking in, rather than inside looking out. They engage in self-focused attention to try and be the right person.'

Of course, a certain amount of self-awareness is important; thinking about how we're presenting to the world, and about other people's feelings, but this is different to being self-conscious. 'It always matters what people think of you,' she says, 'but not to the point you can't go out because you look a certain way or don't know enough about politics. You can't live by what others think because you don't know half the time. The reality is: not everyone does like everyone.' The issue with too much self-focused attention in social situations is that there's then a tendency to withdraw; to stop engaging. 'And this feeds the belief that they're boring,' Argent explains. 'They don't say as much. And the behaviours – through anxiety – self-perpetuate.'

In terms of social anxiety, there's usually a trigger, she explains. 'Then this is followed by a belief: "I'm not going to have a good time". And after this comes panicky symptoms which make them too aware. They think they won't have anything to say. They start overthinking. They're frightened of not saying the right thing, then they start to have symptoms of anxiety. This is when safety behaviours are adopted, but they actually make them more self-conscious: they think about what they're going to say, avoid eye contact.'

So, what can we do to overcome social anxiety?

Judith Argent shared some CBT exercises she uses with patients:

1. Filming yourself

When we're feeling anxious about a social event or exchange – at work, school, with friends, at a party – we have a fear about something happening. So Argent asks the client for a prediction about what might happen if they go and start a conversation with someone and they'll say, for instance: 'I'll look stupid.' So getting them to film themselves is a way of showing them that actually, they don't 'look stupid' when they talk.

2. Trapping

This is about starting to recognise and 'trap' negative thoughts when they appear. So when a fear or negative thought appears, question it. Ask yourself: Am I overthinking this? Am I catastrophising? Sometimes, people might get an image of themselves when they were young, a flashback of sorts. If this happens, you can remind yourself that you are no longer that child. And start to take note of the safety behaviours you slip into, then play with them. In a social environment, consciously adopt all of your safety behaviours; carry them all out. Then try the absolute opposite at another event.

'It's a two-way experiment,' Argent says. 'Noticing the difference.'

3. Shame attacking

Argent might encourage a patient to do or say something silly. 'Patients really enjoy it,' she says. She'll say: What will happen if you do this in public? And asks them to make a prediction. Perhaps they think people will stop and stare. Laugh. She says: And if they do, how will you cope? It's about exploring all eventualities and how it will feel if each did actually happen. 'Almost always, their prediction isn't right. Perhaps people do stare, but it doesn't feel so terrible.' She also encourages them to say something silly with their friends. Again, she asks them to predict what might happen. They might say: My friends will think I'm weird. 'But in reality, when they try it out, their friends may think it's interesting. Or just listen and say "OK". They thought they'd be really judged but often aren't.'

4. Draw yourself blushing

Argent says that people often try safety behaviours to prevent blushing: they stand by a cold window or open door. She challenges their negative judgements, asking: What will happen if you blush? She might then create an environment that's hot, or a situation where they will feel as if they're blushing – get them to talk about something embarrassing – and get them to accept it, to say out loud: 'Oh, I'm blushing.' Rather than thinking it needs to be hidden. 'Blushing doesn't have to mean you're weird and weak and strange. We need people to see themselves blushing to realise it's not so bad; people might not notice, or if they do, they ignore it. Once the patient is blushing Argent asks them to draw how red they think their face is. Or she'll have a paint chart with varying shades of pink and red. Then she'll take a photograph of them or get them to look in the mirror. 'They think they're bright red, but in the photograph or mirror, often it's not as they imagined.'

5. Meet with other shy people

There are social anxiety groups and meet-ups – both online and in person, which Argent suggests looking into, like The Shyness Group. It offers an opportunity to talk to other people who feel similarly, and the groups are self-run. People talk about things they find difficult. There are also social anxiety therapy groups, facilitated by a trained therapist, and they might use video feedback as a group. Or get the group to do 'shame attacking' together; go out in public and do silly things. It can be fun, then.

Argent believes CBT can help anyone with social anxiety. 'It's all about looking at beliefs about how you think you should be. People do so many things – safety behaviours

– which make it worse.' And reassuringly, she says that people can be socially anxious 'but also really successful and coping. Sometimes they might be quiet, feel boring, not funny. But it's about accepting that we're not all like that all the time. Most of us "act as if".' CBT helps by breaking down the negative thoughts and high expectations we have of ourselves and asking what would happen if our fears came true. But also, questions what evidence we have that they will.

What surprised me was how common social anxiety is. Argent has more people coming to see her for social anxiety than anything else, including depression. And she said it's especially common amongst teenagers, which I found both a relief and quite frustrating; I wish I'd known this as a teenager, then I wouldn't have felt so alone with my anxiety. 'There's nothing wrong with having social anxiety,' she said. 'It's about owning it and overcoming it. Throw yourself into it, don't over-monitor. Accept that it's OK to feel like this.'

Most notably, CBT encourages you to face your fear head-on. Don't hide from it or avoid it; go to it, question it, see how it feels. Yahoo's former CEO Marissa Meyer, in an interview with *Vogue*, said that for the first fifteen minutes of any party, she wants to leave – including one in her own home.[5] 'I will literally look at my watch and say, "You can't leave until time x. And if you're still having a terrible time at time x, you can leave."' She faces her fear and, by giving herself permission to leave if her fear is founded and she is having a terrible time, she starts to relax into it. More often than not, she'll end up having a fun time.

9

We need to teach our children that shyness is OK

When I was eight years old, I moved to a new primary school. A few months in, I was sat in assembly and the head teacher announced that I would be singing a solo in front of the whole school. I'd had no time to prepare. So I stood at the front, trembling, as I looked out at around 300 unfamiliar faces. When I starting singing, my voice was so quiet and I didn't know how to make it louder. The head teacher was stood by the piano, saying: 'Louder, louder!'

I now look back and wonder if she was trying to somehow exorcise my shyness. Perhaps she thought that if she forced me to get up in front of all those people and perform, I'd see that it wasn't all that bad – and that would be the end of my shyness. But that's not how it works. I was terrified about being in a new, unfamiliar environment. And I had never performed a solo before. What I needed was patience, kindness and understanding. My shyness wasn't going to be 'cured' by one person's brash actions.

But more importantly, shyness isn't a 'fault' that needs fixing, or something to be cured. And this has become increasingly apparent to me as I've become a mother myself and can see my three children developing their own personalities. Unfortunately, though, nearly three decades after my experience with that head teacher in the school assembly, some adults are still similarly insensitive.

When my daughter, my firstborn, was about ten months old, I took her to a playgroup. I observed as the other babies and toddlers crawled and toddled into the centre of the circle to grab one of the musical instruments that had been splayed out. My daughter stayed with me, on my lap. She didn't want to go. I gently encouraged her, but she wasn't interested. There was a woman sitting next to me, also observing what was going on. I found myself wanting to explain the situation to her, so I said, 'I think she's feeling a bit shy.'

The woman asked, 'Were you shy, as a child?'

I replied, 'Yes, I was, actually.'

And she said, 'That's why your daughter's shy.'

I panicked. I didn't want to be somehow channelling my own childhood shyness into my daughter. But I was also confused: I didn't feel shy now; I enjoyed socialising and putting myself forward in group situations. I wondered how it was that my childhood shyness would somehow transfer. Most importantly, though, it all felt very negative: the way the woman was speaking to me, the judgement she was making, the analysis she was giving. When actually, if my daughter was shy, that wouldn't be a problem. Turns out she isn't; a few months later she started nursery and hasn't stopped talking, performing and displaying outgoing behaviours since. But that's not to say her brothers will be the same.

We had another situation where a neighbour said, of our then two-and-a-half-year-old son: 'Does he ever speak?' He didn't mean it rudely, he was genuinely curious, as our daughter is always so chatty with the neighbours, and our son isn't so much. And again, I took it personally: were we doing something wrong, not to make our son more confident and chatty, like his sister? Was it him who had caught my shyness? But again, it's not helpful for outsiders to diagnose our children, and more importantly, if he is shy sometimes, or talks less in public, that's OK. It's not an issue.

Dr Ruth Erskine says that if she has a child come to see her who is shy, this in itself is not a cause for concern. 'We over-psychologise lots of things,' she says, 'but unless a child can't manage school, for instance, shyness is not a problem.' And if they are struggling at school, this isn't something that the child needs to deal with, it's then down to the teacher to make the environment more welcoming for that child. Dr Erskine remembers a series of sessions she had with a girl who had hearing problems caused by ear infections. 'She was very shy,' Dr Erskine explains. 'She wasn't particularly anxious, but she was reticent; I had to tease her out.' She was about five and had developed a lisp, so felt self-conscious about how she spoke, especially as she was surrounded by articulate girls. Although she was bright, she didn't speak up. 'My advice was for the teacher to enable the child to interact,' she says. 'It's not the child's problem, the environment needs to be manipulated to help her feel confident. She needs to be more nurtured, helped to be part of things.'

This point, in terms of raising a shy child, is crucial: the shyness isn't an issue for the child to fix; it's a trait that should be accepted warmly. Both at home and at school, the child needs to be made to feel comfortable and welcome. But it seems society, and so parents, often feel uncomfortable about having a shy child. Dr Erskine says it depends on how much value the parents put on sociability. 'In our current society, we put value on adaptability because everything is so fast-changing,' she says. 'You want your child to manage in social situations. But various things can lead to a child feeling disheartened: illness, dyslexia, experiencing a knock-back. This can all affect confidence and the child's ability to engage.'

Now a mother myself, I can see how my mum must have felt as the other kids ran off to play and I kept myself close to her; hidden away. That was where I felt safe and protected, but I wonder if there's a biological desire to see your children confidently stride off without you. Once upon a time, it would have been about survival; learning to be independent and to fend for yourself. In our current society, where confidence is celebrated and shyness considered something that needs to be overcome, in many ways it still is.

So I'm grateful that my mum allowed me to move at my own pace. When I talk to her now about my former shyness, she's quick to say: 'You weren't *that* shy; you always had friends. You just sometimes took a while to warm up.' But I distinctly remember the feeling of parting from my dad on a Monday morning, when he dropped me at school, and wanting so much to stay with him rather than enter the bustle of a three-form entry primary school; where the boisterous kids got all the attention and the quiet ones, like me, were left to fend for ourselves.

I also remember the extracurricular activities I was lucky enough to be offered by my parents – ice-skating, ballet, football – but that I felt scared to partake in. Interestingly, the two classes I did stick with well into my teens were piano – one-to-one lessons – and ballet: a calm, slow, non-competitive activity. I wasn't competitive as a child, and I'm not competitive now. I like to work hard and succeed, but it's never about 'winning', it's about proving to myself that I can do it. And this feels very closely linked to my shyness and not wanting to draw attention to myself. So growing up, I often found myself opting out rather than battling to win – in terms of education, friendships, love, sports. If someone else really wanted it, I'd just step back. That was more comfortable to me than confronting my competitor. So it's probably a good job I was never inter-ested in competitive sports, as I might have simply tapped the football over to someone on the other team rather than attempt to do something impressive with it myself.

Dr Emma Svanberg says that as parents, it can be really tempting to push our children forward and tell them 'it's OK, don't be silly'. 'But if we can put ourselves in their shoes, something internal is telling them that they need to stand back and observe before they can feel comfortable to explore.' She says that children's birthday parties are a prime example – some kids will be at the front chatting to the entertainer, others will be sitting on their parents' knees. 'Doing what we can to understand their experience and help them feel comfortable, validating their worry instead of minimising it, can gradually help them feel more confident to explore. But we have to remember that we get the children we get, and any attempt to change something which is fundamentally part of their personality can just leave them feeling misunderstood. Confidence comes from security, not our determination.'

It can be difficult when our parents have one method for supporting us through shyness, but the school has another. Or doesn't have one at all. I remember sitting in classrooms the whole way through school – and university, actually – feeling too shy to put my hand up and answer questions. I wonder how different it would have felt if shyness had been acknowledged in that environment, and spoken about openly. I feel it would have eased my shyness; I might have felt less alone with what I was feeling. This feeling of being 'other' because of my shyness was heightened at secondary school, when at my first parents' evening, my English teacher told my parents that I was 'too quiet'. That I never spoke up in class. That year, I started to feel more confident socially. I started widening my friendship group and became chattier. I began to talk more in class. And that same teacher, at parents' evening the following year, said I talked too much.

How we are treated as children – both in the home and in educational settings – can have a profound impact. Tamu Thomas, who is now in her 40s, remembers being described as a 'crybaby' when she was growing up. 'I remember being very gentle and very wary about rough-and-tumble type play that was normal for most children,' she says. 'I would avoid anything that resembled conflict. I didn't stand up for myself. I experienced some bullying, but in the 80s bullying wasn't assessed in the way it is now, so I internalised it and didn't say much about it because I didn't want to be a crybaby.'

Her dad was very clear that she needed to 'toughen up, stop being so nice and kind because people would take advantage'. She didn't know what that meant, but she knew she shouldn't let it happen. 'He was clear that I would be in big trouble with him if I allowed people to take advantage. I was about six years old.' Her mum responded differently. 'My mum was always full of cuddles and would say that I should tell an adult if other children were unkind,' she remembers.

In trying to be brave and strong, she became guarded and defensive. 'I was never aggressive, but if it seemed like someone was going to take advantage, I would retreat or become aloof,' she says. 'I became very outwardly confident – at times loud – creating an impression of what I thought was tough. It meant that vulnerability became a huge emotional disturbance, and letting people know that I needed them in any way was a big no.' She wasn't unhappy.

She was kind, loving and generous, but if someone made a big deal about it, she would retreat, because acknowledging her kindness felt overwhelming. 'My dad thought he was protecting me,' she says, 'he did what he thought was right – however, his parenting suppressed what have become some of my best characteristics.'

It seems Thomas's father was relaying society's clear message that in order to get ahead, you must be brave and strong, not quiet and careful. And in some ways, this is true. Until we become more accepting of different personalities and needs, the quiet kids will have a harder time of it, because they'll have to fight to be heard, which means battling their instinctive nature. I know, having attended a north London comprehensive secondary school with big classes, lots of misbehaving and no time to nurture the shy children. We were just left to struggle on through. And it was probably presumed that we were simply well-behaved, because we weren't jabbing our peers in the bum with compasses, or setting the classroom alight with Bunsen burners.

Interestingly, shyness in children has been found to be associated with a number of positive behaviours including:

- Doing well at school
- Behaving and not getting into trouble

- Listening attentively to others

- Being easy to look after

And so it's these attributes that we ought to focus on, as parents, rather than feeling as if our children are somehow letting us down by not being the first in line to participate in group activities.

Child and adolescent psychotherapist Laura Fulcher explained the evolutionary neuroscience of shyness to me. 'It's around the age of two that children become shy,' she says, 'because it keeps them safe. It's like with food: fussiness keeps them safe from "poisonous berries".' But this is also the age – two – when children's brains typically grow a lot more rapidly, which is why they start to crave independence and control. 'They think they can do anything because their brain is making so many connections,' she says. 'Then it calms down.' It's then around the age of twelve that it happens again, and it's a lot to deal with. Only this time, they will be starting secondary school and on the brink of puberty, so there are lots of big changes taking place.

'Twelve-year-olds find it very hard to make decisions,' explains Fulcher. 'But they are also very versatile; they have a go at everything. At this age, they see opportunities everywhere – creative, exploratory. But it also feels edgy and dangerous.' As childhood ends and the teenage years begin, they start to explore self-individuation; to work out who they are and who they want to be. This involves trying things out and seeing what works. It's an experimental period. 'But if you feel different to your peers,' explains Fulcher, 'you don't want to do that, so just retire. You think: I don't want to be at this party.'

She says that a lot of shyness is about that. 'In adolescence kids really want to fit in and also find themselves. They want to be in the gang, but that means conforming.' Difference isn't celebrated with young people, she says. 'People are mean about it.'

So what can we do, as parents, to help our children to feel more confident?

'It's all about attachment,' says Fulcher. 'A good attachment with family means you'll feel more confident. Like you can go and conquer the world. If you have a wobbly attachment; if you are not attached, you feel less confident.' She explains that the first seven years are important in terms of establishing a safe and solid foundation – 'the early years are building blocks' – but that we have another chance as teenagers to develop inner confidence.

Popstar and actress Jennifer Lopez shared such a great example of what can happen when we enable our children to try out something new when they are ready, rather than forcing them. It was during a Supersoul Conversations interview with Oprah Winfrey and Lopez described her eleven-year-old daughter Emme asking to be in her video for 'Limitless'.[1] Lopez said that when she was casting girls for the video, Emme overheard her and asked if she could do it. At first Lopez wasn't keen; she didn't want her children to be performing and under pressure. But also, she hadn't considered her daughter for this role, as she was shy.

'She's quiet, you know, she's an angel, a thinker. But she was always quiet. My son is loud and rambunctious and full of energy, and Emme is the opposite: the yin to his yang.'

So she was surprised when Emme asked to be in the video. At first Lopez said no, then she decided to let her give it a go. But she said: 'If you do it, you've got to see it the whole way through.' Emme said 'OK.' And she did it. 'We did the first take, all the way through, and she was a natural. And I look at her and I'm crying . . . like, "Oh my God". And that's when I knew she had "it" . . . she could do whatever she wanted with it.'

With shy children, it's so important to go at their pace and to also take them seriously when they do feel ready to try something, even if we don't imagine them being able to muster the confidence to do it. They need to be given the opportunity to try. And maybe succeed. And possibly fail. But we can't say: I don't think you're ready for this. As that's for them to decide.

Ultimately, it's about accepting our children and their personalities however they unravel. It can be frustrating and emotional to watch our child develop in ways that we think may make integration more challenging for them, but acceptance and nurturing are key. And in terms of shyness, remembering that it may well bestow them with a whole host of attributes that they can tap into later in life. We need to teach our children that it's OK to be shy, but also offer ways to instil confidence.

10
Shyness may come and go

Shyness is a kink in the soul,
a special category, a dimension that
opens out into solitude.

Pablo Neruda

As the pandemic hit, and lockdown was subsequently announced, afflicted countries went into panic mode. Beyond the essential survival needs – food, shelter – many of us wondered how we would get through it, if we couldn't meet friends and family freely. And then we discovered Zoom. But more importantly, for those who remained in good health, and free of financial concerns, there was the re-discovery of time alone and how beneficial it can be to have a quieter life. Social arrangements were replaced with hobbies, yoga, bread-baking, early nights. And for a while, it was rather nice to be free of the burden of plan- and decision-making.

For shy people, it might have been a relief. Psychotherapist Kemi Omijeh explains that if you are naturally a shy person, lockdown will have brought that out in you. 'Perhaps you have adjusted to socialising, working, etc., because you know that society expects that. Lockdown gave you a welcome break from that, no more pretending.' But following the quarantine, we needed to learn to socialise again. 'It will have taken an adjustment and a re-learning post lockdown,' says Omijeh. 'If the individual chose to do this. They may very much just accept their shyness and not readjust.'

But while I was on the fence – both enjoying some quieter time, and also keen to get back to some kind of social normality; Zoom was not for me – I quickly noticed something troubling happening with my children. I'd take my three kids out for our daily morning walk and when we encountered other families with similarly-aged kids – their friends – the kids would stand there awkwardly, not speaking to each other. Where usually, they'd run off and play while the adults talked, now they were mute. Unsure about what was safe. Unable to communicate with their peers, after so much time spent out of these social situations.

Omijeh explains that while adults found lockdown incredibly challenging at times, so did our children. 'Children are not exempt from that overwhelming feeling,' she says. 'And just when they have adjusted to the new normality – something shifts. Bumping into their friends could be part of this shift and they just don't know what to say/do. The awkwardness is a normal/natural response. Uncertainty certainly breeds quietness in children, and there was a lot of uncertainty around, so this will have contributed to how they responded to bumping into their peers. They don't know what to do, how to behave, what the new rules are. And finally, if parents are anything like me, the eagerness to see another adult/parent/friend can put a bit of pressure on. "Oh look it's Jack! Say hi! Go on say hi!" This can lead to the child retreating.'

Omijeh echoes what psychologists Erskine and Svanberg said earlier in the book, which is that shyness as a personality trait isn't something to be concerned about. 'Shyness is often misunderstood because there is an assumption and expectation that the child that is outspoken, chatty, etc., is confident, and the shy child isn't,' she says. 'Shyness as a standalone personality trait is not an issue and doesn't need therapy. However there can be certain events or traumas that happen to a child that lead to shyness. So in my role as therapist, if I get a referral for a "quiet child", my assessment would involve trying to find out whether it's a personality trait or if something has happened. A good indicator of this is that they are usually quiet/shy across all situations and whilst they may be less shy at home, they generally are a "less is more child" in terms of speaking/speaking out.'

In terms of Omijeh's advice for supporting a child going through a shy period, lockdown, or something else that has happened and left them feeling quiet and withdrawn, she advises: 'Patience, planning and playfulness. Go at the child's pace, don't push them, no pressure. Plan and prepare for situations you can – give them forewarning if you can. Playfulness is about having a bit of humour about it to encourage a more relaxed attitude and to ease the pressure. I am not saying mock them, but if you can find humour where you can, use it. With little ones, role play with their toys what happened and what has changed.'

For adults, there might have been conflicting feelings about reintegrating after lockdown. For me, the return of having to make social plans was difficult. I so enjoyed being under no pressure to put dates in the diary. And although I missed social gatherings, I was OK with WhatsApp messaging my friends, and the occasional front garden catch-up. Suddenly, I had to meet with everyone I hadn't seen for a few months, and I slightly dreaded it. Perhaps it was the 'lockholm' syndrome people joked about on social media. Or maybe it was shyness resurfacing. I know that one afternoon I was supposed to meet a neighbour out the front for a cup of tea and catch-up, and all day I was planning my excuse. But fortunately, as the meeting time was upon us, I bumped into her on my way back from the shops. I started talking and couldn't stop. It was so exciting to have adult interaction with someone other than my husband. It is during moments like that that I realise it's shyness, not introversion, that I'm experiencing. And although some friends and family members might find my hesitation about meeting frustrating sometimes, I am learning to accept it is part of my DNA. I can make an effort to hide it, but it doesn't mean I won't feel it. I'm shy. That's all there is to it.

I was interested to hear that my mother, Julia, has experienced bouts of shyness. Even with my 'shydar' out, I'd never picked up on this. She always seems calm and confident, and ready to take on new people and situations. And on the whole, my analysis is right. But she told me that she remembers blushing as a child: 'I always used to blush as a child and it became worse in my teenage years when it would spread all over my neck and chest too. As the years passed and I became more confident and satisfied in my working life I found that I stopped blushing too.'

Then when she became a mother, and had three children under the age of five, she could feel a certain shyness returning. 'I felt I was always apologising for my own existence and on behalf of my young children too,' she says. 'Whilst reading the *Guardian* I saw an advert for an assertiveness course for women, and knew I needed to go on this three-day course. It saved me. I realised that my confidence had just ebbed away. Whenever somebody asked me to do them a favour I felt unable to say no. I then realised how important it is to learn skills to overcome my shyness and lack of confidence. I learned that I didn't always have to answer straight away. I could give myself time to consider and get back to people and say "no", if I wanted to.'

She went on to train as a counsellor and during the training, again realised how difficult she found it to speak in a group setting. 'I discovered that the sooner I spoke the easier it was,' she says, 'especially if I spoke first. I still feel the same now in group situations and try and say my piece first.'

She's now been a therapist for over thirty years. 'Clients often talk about their shyness and their need to overcome it. We explore how this affects them and what they would like to achieve, small steps first. The client will set her own goal and we explore together how she can move towards this aim and discuss how important it is to go at her pace, nobody else's. Also we work together, with the client letting me know how I can support her in moving forward.'

To hear my mother, the same woman who let me hide behind her skirt and never forced me out to socialise before I was ready, but who also appeared so completely at one with herself, describe her own experiences of shyness – both within, and through her clients – is reassuring. It reminds me that as humans, we are imperfect. None of us feels confident all the time. It also highlights the importance of owning our perceived imperfections. If you feel shy, and think it's a fault, I wonder how it would feel instead to own it? Claim it. Announce it. Talk about it.

American professor, lecturer, author, and podcast host Brené Brown speaks such wisdom on shame. She wrote, on her blog: 'I define shame as the intensely painful feeling or experience of believing that we are flawed and therefore unworthy of love and belonging – something we've experienced, done, or failed to do makes us unworthy of connection. I don't believe shame is helpful or productive.'[1]

If shyness is labelled as wrong, or something to overcome, this attaches shame to it. But, as Brené Brown also says, shame cannot survive once you've revealed that thing that you feel ashamed of. So I urge all readers who are shy, and feel ashamed, to tell one friend or family member that you experience shyness. This might feel revealing, or make you feel vulnerable, but it might also help you to feel lighter. You'll no longer be carrying the secret of your shyness.

Mindset coach Rebecca Caution has some lovely words on shyness:

I think shyness needs a rebrand! There is nothing wrong with it and so much right with it. It's a power.

It comes from sensitivity and empathy. These are powers, not weaknesses. Being able to feel the energy of a room full of people means you can really connect with people or decide those people who aren't for you and keep yourself safe. Being able to truly understand another person and connect with their pain or their joy in a meaningful way is at the root of shyness. Shyness is the by-product of that and that ability to connect is the very heart of what it means to be human. How can that be anything but a good thing? If I had been born a child who wasn't shy, my life might have been easier. I might have liked myself more, I might have stepped outside of my comfort zone more and earlier, but I may not have learned these lessons and I wouldn't have the deep empathy and understanding I do for my own shy and sensitive children.

And I agree with Rebecca. If I could go back and remove the shyness from my childhood, would I? I definitely wouldn't. It's an important – even treasured – part of me, and my past. So much so, that when I came across a quote on Instagram that asked: 'What one thing would you never change about yourself?' – I decided that it would be my shyness. It's been there since birth, and it's not going any-where. It will rear its head, sometimes awkwardly, and at other times it will help me to understand how someone else is feeling. But it's no longer something I am wishing away.

Shyness has made me more empathic, more analytical. It makes me a better leader, as a business owner and employer. It makes me a more understanding mother, as I recognise 'difference' in my children – and I encourage them to embrace it rather than fight it. It has taught me, from a young age, that we all face barriers in life, but, when you muster the strength to push through them – and there's always a way – you come out the other side stronger. My shyness has made me stronger.

I invite you to join me in claiming back your own shyness. And when you observe shyness in others, remember that while they may seem cocooned, and somewhat unavailable, there's a beautiful butterfly in there just waiting to come out.

Reference notes

1: Shyness isn't a fixed trait

1 'Does Shyness Vary According to Attained Social Roles? Trends Across Age Groups in a Large British Sample', Nejra Van Zalk, Michael E. Lamb and Peter Jason Rentfrow, *Journal of Personality and Social Psychology*, 85:6, December 2017 (https://onlinelibrary.wiley.com/doi/epdf/10.1111/jopy.12291)

2 'Stability and change of personality across the life course: The impact of age and major life events on mean-level and rank-order stability of the Big Five', J. Specht, B. Egloff, S. C. Schmukle, *Journal of Personality and Social Psychology*, 2011

3 'The science behind why some of us are shy', June 2019 (https://www.bbc.com/future/article/20190604-the-science-behind-why-some-of-us-are-shy)

4 *Coping with Shyness and Social Phobia: A guide to understanding and overcoming social anxiety*, W. Ray Crozier and Lynn E. Alden, Oneworld Publications, 2009

5 'Does Shyness Vary According to Attained Social Roles? Trends Across Age Groups in a Large British Sample', Nejra Van Zalk, Michael E. Lamb and Peter Jason Rentfrow, *Journal*

of Personality and Social Psychology, 85:6, December 2017
(https://onlinelibrary.wiley.com/doi/epdf/10.1111/jopy.12291)

2: Being shy doesn't make you boring

1. 'Does Shyness Vary According to Attained Social Roles? Trends Across Age Groups in a Large British Sample', Nejra Van Zalk, Michael E. Lamb and Peter Jason Rentfrow, *Journal of Personality and Social Psychology*, 85:6, December 2017

2. 'Personality and mate preferences: Five factors in mate selection and marital satisfaction', M. D. Botwin, D. M. Buss, T. K. Shackelford, *Journal of Personality and Social Psychology*, 1997

3. 'Does Shyness Vary According to Attained Social Roles? Trends Across Age Groups in a Large British Sample', Nejra Van Zalk, Michael E. Lamb and Peter Jason Rentfrow, *Journal of Personality and Social Psychology*, 85:6, December 2017

4. 'Personality effects on children's speech in everyday life: Sociability-mediated exposure and shyness-mediated reactivity to social situations', J. B. Asendorpf, G. H. Meier, *Journal of Personality and Social Psychology*, 1993

5. 'Elton John: "I still want my dad's approval"', 14 October 2019 (https://www.bbc.co.uk/news/entertainment-arts-5000 3238)

6. Ibid

7. 'Beyoncé on Her Shy and Awkward Phase', *The Oprah Winfrey Show* (https://www.youtube.com/watch?v=VNJrxkR neak)

3: You can ~~always~~ get what you want (without being loud)

1 'My mother's unconventional parenting lessons', July 2016 (https://www.virgin.com/richard-branson/my- mothers-unconventional-parenting-lessons)

2 'Self-regulation underlies temperament and personality: An integrative developmental framework', J. J. A. Denissen, M. A. G. Van Aken, L. Penke, D. Wood, *Child Development Perspectives*, 2013

3 'Michelle Dockery on why she almost ditched *Downton Abbey*', September 2015 (https://www.independent.ie/ entertainment/television/tv-news/michelle-dockery-on-why-she-almost-ditched-downton-abbey-31521992.html)

4 'Rosa Parks: An American hero', August 2012 (https:// www.independent.co.uk/news/world/americas/rosa-parks-an-american-hero-322291.html)

4: Quiet people are more introspective

1 'Introspection In Psychology: Wundt's Experimental Technique', May 2020 (https://www.verywellmind.com/ what-is-introspection-2795 252)

2 'Thom Yorke: Daydream nation', May 2019 (https://crack magazine.net/article/long-reads/thom-yorke-daydream-nation/)

3 'Ask a Grown Man: Thom Yorke and Nigel Godrich', *Rookie* (https://vimeo.com/63626526?utm_campaign=2617611& utm_source=affiliate&utm_channel=affiliate&cjevent=0eb52 7d4f00b11e 98029003c0a18050b)

5: Shyness can help with your career

1 *A Method to My Quietness: A Grounded Theory Study of Living and Leading with Introversion*, Leatrice Oram (https://pdfs. semanticscholar.org/bb44/80d29fc17b8206ff67139621fbbd 2872a162.pdf?_ga=2.80708439.1764555628.1570533570- 481006571.1570533570)

2 'Is Introversion an Obstacle in Tacit Knowledge Sharing through Socialization? A Study on how Personality Traits Influence Knowledge Sharing Behavior', Anne Karete N. Hvidsten, *Dalhousie Journal of Interdisciplinary Management*, Spring 2016 (https://ojs.library.dal.ca/djim/article/viewFile/ 6442/5821)

3 'The Hidden Advantages of Quiet Bosses', Adam Grant, Francesca Gino and David A. Hofmann, *Harvard Business Review*, December 2010 (https://hbr.org/2010/12/the- hidden-advantages-of-quiet-bosses)

4 'Winning it all: 10 things to learn from Marissa Mayer as a leader', December 2017 (https://yourstory.com/2017/12/10- things-to-learn-from-marissa-mayer-as-a-leader)

5 'What makes Richard Branson a Great Leader?' (https://www. industryleadersmagazine.com/makes-richard-branson-great- leader/)

6 'Mark Zuckerberg's Most Valuable Friend', October 2010 (https://www.nytimes.com/2010/10/03/business/03face.html)

7 'The rise of social media', Ortiz-Ospina, E., September 2019 (https://ourworldindata.org/rise-of-social-media)

6: But confidence helps too

1 'Does Shyness Vary According to Attained Social Roles? Trends Across Age Groups in a Large British Sample', Nejra Van Zalk, Michael E. Lamb and Peter Jason Rentfrow, *Journal of Personality and Social Psychology*, 85:6, December 2017

2 'How Nicole Kidman Got Over Her Shyness While Acting', December 2018 (https://www.backstage.com/magazine/article/nicole-kidman-acting-advice-interview-actors-66388)

3 'Get to know Fleabag's 'hot priest' Andrew Scott', October 2019 (https://www.standard.co.uk/lifestyle/esmagazine/we-get-to-know-fleabags-hot-priest-andrew-scott-a4257091.html)

4 'Does Shyness Vary According to Attained Social Roles? Trends Across Age Groups in a Large British Sample', Nejra Van Zalk, Michael E. Lamb and Peter Jason Rentfrow, *Journal of Personality and Social Psychology*, 85:6, December 2017

5 Ibid

7: The online world is a shy person's friend

1 'Shyness, Internet Use, and Personality', Susan Ebeling-Witte, B.A., Michael L. Frank, Ph.D., and David Lester, Ph.D., *Cyberpsychology & Behavior*, Volume 10, Number 5, 2007

2 'Shyness and Online Social Networking Services', Levi Baker and Debra L. Oswald, *Journal of Social and Personal Relationships 27*, November 2010 (https://www.researchgate.net/publication/49243428_Shyness_and_Online_Social_Networking_Services)

8: You can overcome acute social anxiety

1 *Coping with Shyness and Social Phobia: A guide to understanding and overcoming social anxiety*, W. Ray Crozier and Lynn E. Alden, Oneworld Publications, 2009

2 *The Expression of the Emotions in Man and Animals*, Charles Darwin, ed. Joe Cain and Sharn Messenger, first pub. 1872, this edition pub. Penguin Classic, 2009

3 *Coping with Shyness and Social Phobia: A guide to understanding and overcoming social anxiety*, W. Ray Crozier and Lynn E. Alden, Oneworld Publications, 2009

4 Ibid

5 'Yahoo's Marissa Mayer: Hail to the Chief', August 2013 (https://www.vogue.com/article/hail-to-the-chief-yahoos-marissa-mayer)

9: We need to teach our children that shyness is OK

1 'Oprah and Jennifer Lopez: Your Life in Focus', *The Oprah Winfrey Podcast* (https://www.youtube.com/watch?v=uGrpYL yzH14)

10: Shyness may come and go

1 'shame v. guilt', January 2013 (https://brenebrown.com/blog/2013/01/14/shame-v-guilt/#:)

Acknowledgements

Grandma Mary. You were quiet, patient and kind. I now understand that you were shy, too. The perfect example of how shyness can be an attribute.

Mum and dad. Thank you for loving me, supporting me and never trying to 'cure' my shyness.

Rich: you're not sure about shyness. So you better read this book. But thank you for believing in me and my dreams.

Joni, my firstborn. You inspire me daily with your creativity, intelligence and beautiful nature.

Bodhi, my middle kid. Your quiet confidence is your secret weapon. You'll realise this as you get older.

Rudi, 'the baby'. I wrote this book while you slept in a bouncer at my side. It was a magical time.

To all at 4th Estate and Harper Collins. Thank you, so much, for continuing to support me and my writing. I'm honoured to be one of your authors.

Naomi Mantin, you're the best publicist. Thank you for lining up the dreamiest PR opportunities.

To all the psychologists and psychotherapists who kindly shared their knowledge for this book: thank you. You played an integral part in making this book what it is.

And, of course, to all the intelligent, creative and fascinating shy people who shared their stories. It was so inspiring, hearing about how you work it.

Lastly – and most importantly – Michelle Kane. My editor, publisher and friend. Without you, none of this would have happened. You're always open to new ideas, you listen intently and you give the best advice. Thank you so very, very much.